Guitar Rhythm & Technique

FOR

DUMMIES®

A Wiley Brand

by Desi Serna

FOR

DUMMIES®

A Wiley Brand

Guitar Rhythm & Technique For Dummies®

Published by:
John Wiley & Sons, Inc.,
111 River Street, Hoboken,
NJ 07030-5774,
www.wiley.com

For general information on our other products and services, please contact our Customer Care Department within the U.S. at 877-762-2974, outside the U.S. at 317-572-3993, or fax 317-572-4002. For technical support, please visit www.wiley.com/techsupport.

Wiley publishes in a variety of print and electronic formats and by print-on-demand. Some material included with standard print versions of this book may not be included in e-books or in print-on-demand. If this book refers to media such as a CD or DVD that is not included in the version you purchased, you may download this material at http://booksupport.wiley.com. For more information about Wiley products, visit www.wiley.com.

Library of Congress Control Number: 2014958346

ISBN 978-1-119-02287-9 (pbk); ISBN 978-1-119-02288-6 (ebk); ISBN 978-1-119-02289-3 (ebk)

Manufactured in the United States of America

10 9 8 7 6 5 4 3 2 1

Contents at a Glance

Table of Contents

Introduction

Rhythm is the pace and pattern of a piece of music. Technique is the procedure and skill used to sound notes. *Guitar Rhythm & Technique For Dummies* is where you get a grip on keeping time and hone your guitar-playing chops so that you play music well and progress to new levels.

About This Book

This book covers a wide array of rhythm and technique topics, with focus on the most used and most practical skills. You get a grip on keeping time and playing strum patterns, as well as reading and counting basic rhythms. Your fretting-hand fingers get in shape by working with guitar articulations such as hammer-ons, pull-offs, slides, and bends, and you explore various ways in which you can finger chords and fret scales in order to play to your strengths. On the other hand (literally), you work with various methods of flatpicking, fingerpicking, and hybrid picking — skills that add variety to your playing. You also produce harmonics, play in alternate tunings, use a slide, and work with a tremolo system. Throughout the entire book you see references to popular songs and familiar artists, which helps you connect the concepts to the music you know and love — the types of songs you regularly hear on Top 40 and classic-rock radio stations.

The traditional approach to rhythm usually emphasizes all the aspects of standard musical notation and covers the gamut of note values and time signatures. This book focuses only on what you need to know in order to play popular strum patterns and read the most basic of rhythm charts. Instead of making you work to develop advanced skills at high levels of proficiency, this book serves as an overview of the most practical of guitar techniques that are common to popular styles and useful to increasing your versatility.

Here's what sets this book apart from other guitar resource materials:

- ✔ **The practicality and efficiency of the content:** If you don't need to know a certain topic or technique to play guitar and understand popular music, I don't present it here.

- ✔ **The number of familiar song references:** Say goodbye to learning abstract ideas without knowing how they apply to the music you know and love! I refer to some of the most popular songs and famous guitarists of all time in the pages that follow.

As you work your way through this book, keep in mind that sidebars and Technical Stuff icons are skippable. Here are a few other things to note:

- ✔ All the information applies to both acoustic and electric guitar unless otherwise noted.

- ✔ I use six-string guitars and standard tuning in all examples and figures unless otherwise noted.

- ✔ You can apply much of the information in the book to bass guitar, too.

- ✔ I use a right-hander's perspective throughout the book.

- ✔ You have to look up and practice popular song references on your own. I don't include the music here. (If you're not sure where to find the music for a given song referenced in the text, check out www.musicdispatch.com, www.musicnotes.com, or www.sheetmusicplus.com.)

Within this book, you may note that some web addresses break across two lines of text. If you're reading this book in print and you want to visit one of these web pages, simply key in the web address exactly as it's noted in the text, pretending as though the line break doesn't exist. If you're reading this as an e-book, you've got it easy — just click the web address to go directly to the web page.

Before beginning the book, be sure to get your fingers and guitar prepared for optimal playing. Make sure the nails on your fretting hand are trimmed and filed so that they don't interfere with your fretting of the strings. Also, make sure that your guitar has been professionally set up so that it's easy to play and stays in tune.

Finally, in case you're curious, I use the programs GuitarPro (www.guitar-pro.com), Neck Diagrams (www.neckdiagrams.com), and Sibelius (www.sibelius.com) to create notation and diagram figures.

Foolish Assumptions

This book is geared toward experienced beginners and intermediate guitar players. At the very least, you need to know the basics of guitar playing. You should have completed a beginner-level course, like *Guitar For Dummies,* and be able to play your way through many simple songs. Advanced guitarists can benefit from this book by filling in gaps that may have been overlooked over the years and sharpening skills that were never given the proper attention they deserve.

Whatever the case may be, to get the full benefit of this book, you need to know and be able to play and read the following:

- Open chords and open-chord songs
- Power chords and power-chord songs
- Barre chords and barre-chord songs
- Some melodies and riffs
- Guitar tab and neck diagrams

You don't need to be an expert on these concepts; you just need a working knowledge of them. You don't have to know how to read standard musical notation, either, because what you need to know about the staff is covered.

If you still need to learn the basics and acquire the skills listed here, I suggest you start with *Guitar For Dummies,* by Mark Phillips and Jon Chappell (Wiley).

Icons Used in This Book

In order to highlight different types of information, I mark certain paragraphs with the following icons:

The Tip icon points out tips, tricks, shortcuts, and more that make your life as a guitar player a little easier.

The Remember icon points out especially important concepts that you don't want to miss or forget.

The Technical Stuff icon highlights technical information (go figure!) that you can skip if you're short on time (or if you just want to focus on the need-to-know stuff).

The Play This icon points out the audio tracks and video clips I've recorded to illustrate various rhythms and techniques throughout the book.

Beyond the Book

As if all the great information in this book weren't enough, you can go beyond the book for even more!

I've recorded numerous audio tracks and video clips so that you can listen to and view various rhythms, techniques, and more throughout the book. Go to `www.dummies.com/go/guitarrhythmtechnique` to download these files.

Be sure to check out the free Cheat Sheet at `www.dummies.com/cheatsheet/guitarrhythmtechnique` for all sorts of super-handy info, including a rhythm pyramid, finger exercises, and a warm-up routine.

Finally, you can find articles on following a lead sheet, singing and playing at the same time, getting the U2 sound, using a capo, and using accompaniment and tracks at `www.dummies.com/extras/guitarrhythmtechnique`.

Where to Go from Here

As with all *For Dummies* books, you don't have to read this book from beginning to end. You can start anywhere you like. However, because some musical concepts build on others, you won't be able to jump into some lessons without knowing what comes before them. For example, you can't read and play eighth- and sixteenth-note strum patterns in Chapters 3 and 4 until after you get to know the music staff and note values in Chapter 2. That said, Parts I and II focus on reading and playing rhythms, primarily strum patterns and keeping time. Parts III and IV focus on techniques, primarily how you use your hands to manipulate the strings and sound notes. Part V puts everything in the book to good use through exercises and practice routines. Part VI gives you a little something extra to work on before you finish up.

You don't need to learn and master every technique covered in this book. Pick and choose which techniques to focus on. Even the pro players mentioned in these pages have special areas of expertise. For example, Eddie Van Halen's trademark technique is finger tapping, while Bonnie Raitt prefers to sound notes by using a slide. Each of these artists plays to his or her strengths and in ways that best suit his or her style. You may choose to focus on techniques that apply best to acoustic guitar, if that's your preferred platform. You may focus on techniques heard in rock guitar solos if that's the area in which you want to improve.

As you work through this book, work with each concept one at a time. Take breaks from the text to practice and rehearse what you read about. Your goal is to commit a skill to both your mental memory and your hand memory before reading on and playing more. With some concepts, you may learn them after only a few minutes of practice; others may take hours. Take as much time as you need to practice playing and rehearsing the topics I cover here. This isn't a race. Enjoy the process and make everything stick — that is, work with the concepts until they become a permanent part of your playing.

It's not enough to play something new off a page in this book. You need to play each rhythm and technique in context (that is, in actual songs) to really understand what to do with it. That's why I reference so many songs throughout this book. You don't need to look up and learn every single song I mention, but try to play through a few examples every time you learn a new concept. You don't have to learn every song in its entirety, either. If I reference a song because it features a specific strum pattern, then just focus on playing that part of it. If my focus is on a particular technique, then just play through the part that features it.

Part I

Getting Started with Guitar Rhythm and Technique

In this part . . .

✔ Find out how to use a metronome as a pacesetter and to develop rock-solid timing.

✔ Get to know the most basic parts of the music staff so that you can find your way around a lead sheet.

✔ Work with note values, rests, and time signatures to play strum patterns and develop your rhythm-guitar skills.

Chapter 1

Rhythm and Technique in a Nutshell

In This Chapter

▶ Getting an overview of rhythm and technique

▶ Access the audio tracks and video clips at www.dummies.com/go/guitarrhythmtechnique

I n this chapter, I explain why it's beneficial for you to develop your sense of rhythm and sharpen your technique. I also give you an overview of the different topics you explore as you work through this book. When you have an idea of what the whole program is about, you have a clearer picture of the road that lies ahead.

Recognizing the Importance of Rhythm and Technique

Every aspect of guitar playing requires some level of skill. As much as you might like to jump straight to playing familiar songs by your favorite bands and improvising like your favorite guitarists, the truth is that you need to work on developing your technique before you can achieve success on your instrument. Sure, you can pick up on things here and there as you go, but if you're serious about getting good, why not take a more purposeful approach, one that produces better results in a shorter amount of time? The progress of many guitarists is hindered not because they lack the ability to play well, but because they don't follow the steps necessary to progress. How can you sound as good as the next person when the next person has learned tips and tricks that you haven't yet been introduced to?

All guitarists, regardless of style, make use of the same basic techniques. How much you use a particular technique, or how far you take it, is a matter of preference and part of what defines your sound and style.

You can get a taste of what rhythm and technique is all about by watching Video Clip 1 and listening to Audio Track 1.

Reading and Playing Basic Rhythms

Your journey to improving your guitar playing starts with a look at rhythms. *Rhythm* is the time in which you sound notes. It affects the feel and groove of everything you play. Developing your rhythm doesn't require you to read music like a concert violinist, but it's helpful to get to know the basic components of a staff and how music is rhythmically notated, which is precisely what Chapter 2 focuses on. This information will not only help you to improve your strumming, but also prepare you to read the slash notation commonly used in performance charts.

Developing Your Strumming Technique

In this book, you work with some aspects of standard notation strictly as a means to improve your guitar playing. Seeing how measures of music are subdivided, counted, and strummed will take the guesswork out of your rhythm playing and help you get your pick-strokes in order.

Aside from dissecting the strum patterns used in popular music, you work with developing essential rhythm guitar skills such as floating, resting, damping, scratching, and accenting. These techniques contribute to the feel and sound of a rhythm part and help you to develop a strong groove whether you're playing folky acoustic guitar songs, electric rock rhythms, or funky chord comps. Various rhythms, strum patterns, and strumming techniques are covered in Chapters 3, 4, and 5.

Honing Your Fretting-Hand Techniques

There is far more to the left hand (or the right hand if you're a lefty) than simply fretting notes on the fretboard. Guitarists use fretting-hand fingers to hammer into notes as well as pull off, slide, and bend. These techniques, called *articulations,* help you execute passages, produce unique sounds, and be more expressive. In order to advance as a player and be successful as a musician, you need to develop these performance skills and know how they're notated in a guitar score. You work with articulations at length in Chapter 7.

In addition to developing technique, you also need to know how to play to your strengths. Perhaps some of your struggles are caused by a belief that there are "proper" and "correct" ways that things should be played on guitar. The truth is, your hands don't work in exactly the same way as someone else's hands, and sometimes you need to explore unconventional ways to fret and finger chord shapes and scale patterns in order to find what best suits you. You get started with this process in Chapter 6.

Honing Your Picking-Hand Techniques

There is far more to the right hand (or the left hand if you're a lefty) than simply brushing the strings. To reach any level of proficiency with guitar, you need to develop the techniques of picking with a flatpick (also known as a plectrum) and plucking with the fingers.

Skilled players alternate their picks, synchronize their hands, cleanly sound notes, and mute idle strings — all at the same time. When you break down the mechanics of picking alone, you see that various means of picking exist — including alternate, sweep, economy, inside, outside, cross, and hybrid (all techniques covered in Chapter 10).

Popular music features guitar parts that are played using both a pick and fingers. All guitarists put down the pick from time to time and opt to pluck strings using fingers. Led Zeppelin's "Stairway to Heaven," one of the most famous guitar compositions ever, opens with a fingerpicked acoustic guitar. Many folk-inspired songs, like "Dust in the Wind" by Kansas, are propelled by rhythmic patterns that are fingerpicked, not strummed.

Using fingers also lends well to styles where chords and melodies are played together. In some cases, a flatpick is held and used together with fingers for a hybrid of the two methods. In other cases, the picking hand is used to slap the strings and produce percussive sounds. All these techniques are explored in Chapter 11.

Using Whammy Bars

Playing guitar isn't always about manipulating the strings with your hands. Sometimes a piece of hardware is involved, like a tremolo system, which is a spring-loaded bridge that is used to add vibrato, as well as dive away from and scoop into notes. It's what Stevie Ray Vaughan used to add mellow vibrato on his song "Lenny," and what Jimi Hendrix used to conjure up the sounds of bombs and ambulance sirens in his Woodstock performance of "The Star-Spangled Banner." Also called a *whammy bar,* the arm that extends from a tremolo system can be pushed and pulled to create faux-slide guitar sounds with notes that slide up and down, into and out of pitch. All these techniques are laid out for you in Chapter 12.

Playing Slide Guitar and Using Open Tunings

Sometimes guitarists don't fret notes in the normal manner of pressing the strings down to the fretboard using their fingertips; instead, they use a glass or metal object to slide along the tops of the strings. Think of the signature guitar riff at the beginning of Lynyrd Skynyrd's "Free Bird" or anything by Bonnie Raitt. These objects, called *slides,* are usually worn over a fretting-hand finger, and their use is commonplace in popular music.

One of the things that helps to facilitate the use of a slide is an *alternate tuning* (anything that differs from standard tuning). Slide players usually opt to tune the strings so that the open strings produce a chord like E major or G major. These tunings can be used with or without a slide. You get to know them in Chapter 9.

Getting Your Practice In

Any good book on rhythm and technique provides exercises useful for getting the most out of your practice time. Throughout this book, you come across countless figures to rehearse and use for developing your newfound skills. Chapter 13 is geared toward reviewing and running down your rhythms, and it does so in a manner that will make you feel more confident the next time you're called to perform a part by reading it off a rhythm chart. In Chapter 14, melodic patterns are introduced. Sometimes called *scale sequences* or *picking patterns,* these patterns not only provide melodic ideas that are useful when improvising and composing, but also serve as some of the best exercises to sharpen your picking, fretting, and hand synchronization.

Chapter 2

Getting to Know the Music Staff and Traveling through Time

In This Chapter

▶ Finding the beat

▶ Playing quarter notes, half notes, and whole notes

▶ Getting to know time signatures

▶ Access the audio tracks and video clips at www.dummies.com/go/guitarrhythmtechnique

In this chapter, you take your first baby steps toward reading and playing rhythms. You get to know the music staff and some of its basic components. You begin playing quarter notes, half notes, whole notes, dots, and ties, and work with time signatures and metronomes. All this information is elementary-level stuff and, honestly, not very exciting, but you need to know it in order to play the much cooler strum patterns and rhythmic ideas in Chapters 3, 4, and 5.

Keeping Your Finger on the Pulse

Before you even take a look at rhythms on a staff, you get to know how time works in music. Every song is guided by a steady pulse. The pulse itself is not always present in the music — that is, it's not normally assigned to an instrument to play — but everything in the music follows it and it holds everything together. Musicians are seen internalizing this pulse by tapping their feet, nodding their heads, or rocking and swaying their bodies.

Players are introduced to the pulse during a *count-in* or *count-off,* when a band leader calls out numbers prior to the start of a song. This counting serves three purposes:

✔ It establishes the *tempo* of a song (how fast or slow the music moves along).

✔ It indicates the *time signature* (how the music is segmented and counted).

✔ It cues the players to all start together (preventing train wrecks).

When a pulse is established, the band members keep it silently in their heads and use it as a guide while playing their parts.

Although pulses are usually internalized, musicians often use mechanical and electronic devices to keep a steady pulse for their reference. A *metronome* is any device that produces a regular, metrical sound. The sound is a tick, click, beep, or any other, usually percussive, sound that is clearly audible during performance and distinguishable from the instrumentation. Whatever sound is used, musicians commonly refer to it as the *click*.

When a click track is in use during a live performance or recording session, it's piped to musicians via headphones so that it isn't heard by the listeners and doesn't interfere with the actual music. In this day and age, aside from keeping the time steady, click tracks are often necessary to sync live performances to additional audio, video, lights, lasers, heck, even explosions! Because drummers are the timekeepers of the bands, and other instrumentalists follow their lead, click tracks are often added only to the drummers' headphone mixes.

In the old days, a metronome consisted of an adjustable weight on the end of an inverted pendulum rod. You may have seen one of these pyramid-shaped mechanical devices sitting on top of a piano. The pendulum swings back and forth at a specified rate, while a mechanism inside the metronome produces a clicking sound with each oscillation. Nowadays, metronomes keep time and produce sounds electronically. Stand-alone, electronic metronomes are similar in size and appearance to electronic guitar tuners. Metronomes also come built into keyboards, drum machines, and music-recording software programs. Even some guitar amps, particularly the digital variety, offer a metronome feature. You can download metronome apps and use them on your smartphone or tablet. Prerecorded metronome clicks, called *click tracks,* are available on CD or as MP3 and WAV downloads at various tempos.

You can hear a sample metronome sound in Audio Track 2.

You work with metronome click tracks throughout all of *Guitar Rhythm & Technique For Dummies* — some provided for you in the audio and video examples, and others that you need to generate with your own device. If you don't have a metronome, buy or borrow one now!

When figures in this book don't include tempo markings, that means the tempos aren't important and you can play at any rate that's comfortable for you.

Drawn and Quartered

The pulse I mention in the previous section is commonly thought of and counted in groups of four. This is why a count-in is called out as "One, two, three, four." In music, each pulse is called a *beat* and each group of four is called a *measure* or a *bar.* Each of the four beats in a measure takes up one-quarter of it, just as four quarters make a dollar. In written music, these *quarter notes* (formally referred to as *crotchets*) are symbolized with a filled-in oval note head and a straight, flagless stem. Figure 2-1 shows an example of four bars of quarter notes.

Figure 2-1: Quarter notes.

© John Wiley & Sons, Inc.

Click tracks often feature a unique sound on the first of every four clicks. This reminds players that the music is in a 4/4 time signature and helps them keep track of beat one, the first beat of each new measure.

In the following sections, you get to know the components of a music staff, begin to read basic rhythms, and deal with ways in which written music is simplified for guitarists.

If you would like to make your own guitar tablature and notation, get the program GuitarPro (www.guitar-pro.com) or Sibelius (www.sibelius.com).

Rhythmic notation

Sometimes using full-blown standard musical notation isn't necessary, and an alternate style of notation called *rhythmic notation* is used to simplify a score, especially when the score is relied upon mainly for its rhythmic markings. In rhythmic notation, the oval note heads are converted to slashes that are centered on the middle staff line; in some cases, only one staff line is used, as shown in Figure 2-2. You work with mainly rhythmic notation throughout the sections of this book that focus on rhythm.

Figure 2-2: Rhythmic notation.

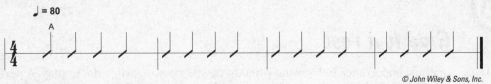

© John Wiley & Sons, Inc.

Beats per minute

The first thing you see in the upper-left corner of Figure 2-2 is a small quarter note followed by an equal sign and the number 80. This indicates the *tempo* with the number 80 indicating that the quarter notes are played at 80 *beats per minute* (BPM). The higher the BPM, the quicker the pulse and tempo. The lower the BPM, the slower the pulse and tempo. 60 BPM is a quarter note every second. 30 BPM is a quarter note every two seconds. 120 BPM is a quarter note every half second. Don't bother getting your stopwatch out to determine the proper tempo for 80 BPM — that's what your metronome is for! All metronomes operate by adjusting and setting the BPM.

Time signature

The next thing you see in Figure 2-2 is a fraction, with a 4 over a 4. That's the *time signature*. The number on the bottom tells you how many beats are in each measure, and the number on top tells you what kind of note value gets counted as one beat. In this case, there are four beats to a measure and quarter notes are counted as the beats. No surprise here — you know that there are four quarter notes per measure, but in some cases, which you explore a little later in this section and again in Chapter 5, measures are divided by less or more than four beats, and another note value, such as the eighth note, is counted as the beat. For now, though, you stick with a 4/4 time signature, also known as *common time* and sometimes indicated with a c symbol rather that the 4-over-4 fraction.

Bar lines

The next thing to notice in Figure 2-2 are the bar lines, which are the vertical lines separating each measure. The double bar line followed by a thicker bar line at the end signifies — you guessed it — the end!

Chords

The last thing to notice about Figure 2-2 is the letter A above the first beat of the first measure. This indicates what pitch or chord to play. I chose A just to give you something to play. At this time, it's not important what type of A chord you play, so you can play any type including an open A chord, an A barre chord, or an A power chord. You can even play just the root, A, using the fifth fret of the sixth string, or the open fifth string.

Each quarter note in Figure 2-2 corresponds to a click from a metronome or click track. You can set your device to 80 BPM and practice playing along by strumming the A at precisely the same time as each click, or go back to and follow Audio Track 2.

All the examples in this chapter are played using an A chord, but you can try practicing them on your own with a metronome using any type of note or chord you like.

Give it a rest

Of equal importance to knowing when to play is knowing when *not* to play. A period of silence is called a *rest*. A quarter note rest looks like a vertical squiggly line and is equal in duration to a quarter note: one beat. Figure 2-3 features four bars of quarter-note rests. Each rest corresponds to a click and signifies that you keep quiet. Just to be sure that you're on the right track (so to speak), resting doesn't mean that the pulse stops, it means that you keep quiet while the beats and measures continue to progress.

Figure 2-3: Quarter-note rests.

© John Wiley & Sons, Inc.

In Figure 2-4, you begin to play something with rhythmic variation to it. Here you sound A (in any manner you like) for each quarter note, and you silence the strings for every quarter-note rest. During periods of rest, you can cut off the string vibrations by lifting your fretting-hand fingers slightly from the fretboard, lowering a part of your picking hand onto the strings, or a combination of both.

Notice at the end of Figure 2-4 that the double bar line has two dots to the left of it. That's a *repeat sign,* and it directs you back to the beginning for another pass. You hear Figure 2-4 in Audio Track 3. After the repeat, I drop out and let the click track resume for some time, giving you an opportunity to practice by yourself.

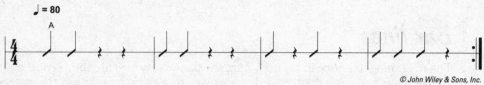

Figure 2-4: Quarter notes and rests 80 BPM.

© John Wiley & Sons, Inc.

When you get the hang of following Figure 2-4, you can try longer examples at faster tempos. Figure 2-5 (Audio Track 4) mixes quarter notes with quarter-note rests for a full 16 measures, with the rest placed on a different beat in every set of four bars, and all at a new tempo of 90 BPM. Figure 2-6 (Audio Track 5) further mixes the quarter notes and rests and at a rate of 100 BPM. All three audio tracks leave enough click track at the end for you to practice on your own.

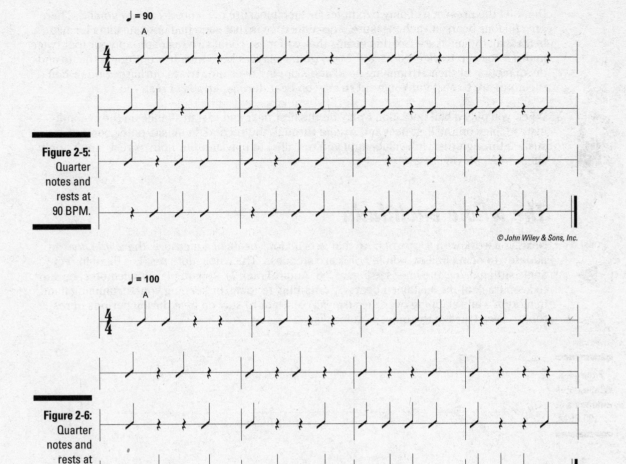

Figure 2-5:
Quarter notes and rests at 90 BPM.

Figure 2-6:
Quarter notes and rests at 100 BPM.

Knowing the half of it

You can play one beat at a time, but what happens if you want to sustain a note for a longer period of time? One option is to play a *half note*. As the name implies, a half note takes up half a measure, or two beats. Half notes look like hollowed-out quarter notes. The *half-note rest*, a filled-in rectangle sitting on top of the middle line of the musical staff, or in the middle of the line in my slash notation examples, takes up two beats as well (see Figure 2-7 and play along with Audio Track 6).

Figure 2-7:
Half notes and rests at 100 BPM.

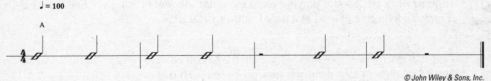

Don't let the presence of only two notes in each measure of Figure 2-7 throw you off. There are still four beats in each measure. The difference is that each half note sustains for two beats, half the measure. So, this means that you must count two beats or tap your foot twice in order to keep track of the beats. Many guitar players keep time by continuing the up-and-down motion of their strumming hand and skipping over the strings during periods when the notes are to sustain. You want to stay on beat during periods of rest, too.

When you play a half note, don't play on the first beat and rest in silence on the second. Instead, play on the first beat and *sustain* through the second. In music, notes continue to sustain through their full value, until you're called to play another note or rest. You're only silent when playing a rest.

The whole enchilada

Next, you work with a type of note that gets all four beats of a measure, the *whole note.* In addition to being hollow, whole notes are stemless. The whole-note rest is a filled-in rect-angle sitting *below* the line (see Figure 2-8; Audio Track 7). As you play whole notes, be sure to keep track of the sustained beats by counting, tapping, or keeping your strumming hand in motion while skipping over the strings. You want to stay on beat during periods of rest, too, so keep track of the pulse in some way.

Figure 2-8:
Whole notes and rests at 100 BPM.

© John Wiley & Sons, Inc.

Fit to be tied

Another way to increase the length of a note is to join it to another note. In music, this is done by using a curved line called a *tie* that connects two note heads of the same pitch. When two quarter notes are tied together, you strike the first note and let it sustain through both its value and the value of the next. For example, a pair of quarter notes tied together are equal to a half note. Two half notes tied together are equal to a whole note. A quarter note and half note tied together are sustained for three beats. Notes can even be tied from measure to measure (see Figure 2-9; Audio Track 8).

Mix and mingle

Now that you know quarter, half, and whole notes, plus their corresponding rests, it's time to work with some playing exercises that mix everything up. See Figure 2-10 (Audio Track 9), which is played at a new tempo of 120 BPM.

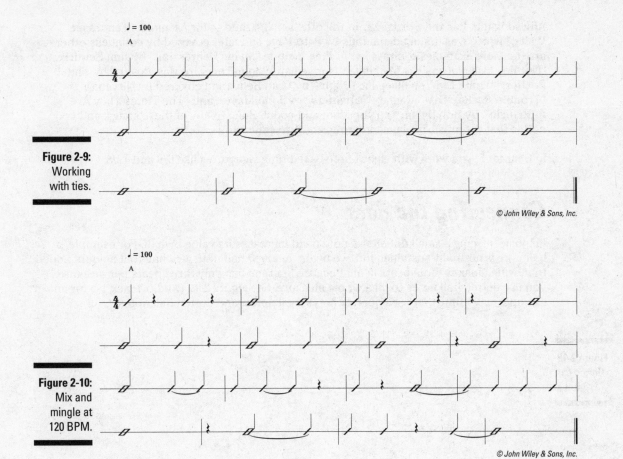

Figure 2-9:
Working
with ties.

© John Wiley & Sons, Inc.

Figure 2-10:
Mix and
mingle at
120 BPM.

© John Wiley & Sons, Inc.

Playing in 3/4 time

Music is commonly played in 4/4 time, but other types of time signatures exist. Figure 2-11 (Audio Track 10) gives you a look at music in 3/4 time. In 3/4 time, you have only three quarter notes, or three beats, per measure. You count it 1 2 3, 1 2 3, and so on. 3/4 time is also called a *waltz,* because the dance by the same name is done to music in triple meter. In waltz time, the count-in is often done twice like this: "1 2 3, 1 2 3, begin." This gives you a little extra time to get acquainted with the shorter measures and triple meter. Notice in Audio Track 10 that the first beat of each measure is still emphasized.

Figure 2-11:
Waltz in 3/4
time.

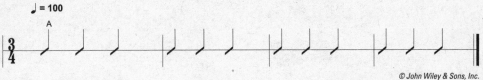

© John Wiley & Sons, Inc.

Any song that has the word *waltz* in the title is in 3/4 time — for example, "Tennessee Waltz," which was first made famous by Patti Page and later covered by countless other artists. More examples of songs in 3/4 time include "Manic Depression" by Jimi Hendrix, "Nothing Else Matters" by Metallica, "Norwegian Wood (This Bird Has Flown)" by The Beatles, "Where Did You Sleep Last Night" by Lead Belly (and covered by Nirvana), "Trouble" by Ray LaMontagne, "Daughters" by John Mayer, and "The Times They Are A-Changin'" by Bob Dylan. Tap your foot and count along to any of these songs, and you notice that the music is played in groups of three pulses.

In Chapter 5, you work with eighth-note-based time signatures like 6/8 and 12/8.

Connecting the dots

In music, placing a small dot after a note head increases its value by half. For example, a half note is normally sustained for two beats. A *dotted* half note gets half that amount added to it, which makes three beats in all. Because 3/4 time has only three beats per measure, you use dotted half notes to fill a whole measure. See Figure 2-12 (Audio Track 11) for an example in 3/4 time that uses quarter notes, half notes, and dotted half notes.

Figure 2-12:
Dotted half notes.

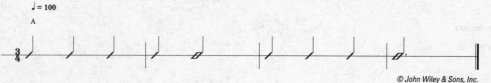

Part II
Reading Rhythms and Strumming Patterns

In this part . . .

✔ Strum the eighth- and sixteenth-note patterns heard in popular music.

✔ Use damping and scratching to enhance the groove.

✔ Play in the style of familiar songs and prepare yourself for gigging.

✔ Work with triplets, shuffles, and compound time signatures as heard in blues-based music.

Chapter 3

Playing Eighth-Note Strum Patterns

* *

In This Chapter

▶ Working with eighth notes

▶ Strumming popular patterns

▶ Damping and scratching the strings

▶ Access the audio tracks and video clips at www.dummies.com/go/guitarrhythmtechnique

* *

*I*n Chapter 2, I introduce you to the basic components of the music staff, and you play simple rhythms. In this chapter, you move on to eighth notes and strum patterns that are common to popular music. You work with exercises and techniques designed to develop your sense of rhythm and sharpen your strumming skills.

Getting Behind the Eight Ball

In Chapter 2, you work with quarter notes, which are notes placed on each beat (or each pulse) of a measure in common time, 4/4. When each of these four notes is split in two, you end up with a total of eight notes called, appropriately enough, *eighth notes*. Each eighth note takes up — you guessed it — one eighth of the measure.

Eighth notes look like quarter notes with their filled-in note heads, but they also have *flags* at the tops of their stems. In Figure 3-1, you see a measure of quarter notes followed by a measure of eighth notes, twice. In the first measure of eighth notes (measure two in the example), the flags are hanging from each stem. In the second measure of eighth notes (measure four in the example), the same flags are connecting the eighth-note stems. When the flags connect, they're called *beams*.

Eighth notes can be written with either flags or beams. Flags hang. Beams connect in pairs of two or four.

The formal name for the eighth note is the *quaver*.

Downbeats and upbeats

When the quarter note is split in two to make two eighth notes, so is the beat. The first half of the beat is called the *downbeat;* it's where your foot goes down while tapping. The second part of the beat is called the *upbeat;* it's where your foot comes up while tapping. You know when you play eighth notes correctly because the first note of every pair is directly on the click, and the second note of every pair is opposite the click. Eighth notes are evenly spaced throughout the measure.

Figure 3-1:
Eighth
notes.

© John Wiley & Sons, Inc.

The downbeats are counted 1, 2, 3, 4. The upbeats are called "and." To save space, Figure 3-1 uses the ampersand (&) symbol instead of writing out the word *and*. Eighth notes are counted "1 and 2 and 3 and 4 and."

Take your pick

As you play eighth notes, you need a plan for your picking hand. You pick eighth notes in two ways:

- ✔ You double the rate at which you pick down, sounding notes with downstrokes on both the downbeats and the upbeats. See the downward-pointing arrows in Figure 3-2.

- ✔ You pick at the same rate as quarter notes but strike the string on the way up, too (on the upbeats). See the downward- and upward-pointing arrows in Figure 3-3.

You can see and hear both methods of strumming eighth notes in Video Clip 2.

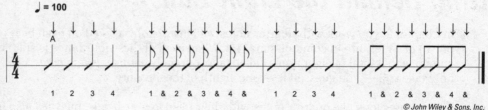

Figure 3-2:
Eighth notes
with down-
strokes.

© John Wiley & Sons, Inc.

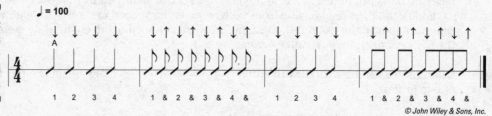

Figure 3-3:
Eighth notes
with down-
strokes and
upstrokes.

© John Wiley & Sons, Inc.

Many songs feature rhythm guitarists strumming straight eighth notes with little to no break in their picking, often opting to use all downstrokes. A few good examples include "Peggy Sue" by Buddy Holly, "Born to Run" by Bruce Springsteen, and "Keep Your Hands to Yourself" by The Georgia Satellites. Bassists do this, too; listen to "With or Without You" by U2 for an example.

Rule of thumb (and fingers)

This book is written with the assumption that you're using a pick (also known as a flatpick or plectrum). I won't cover the basics of holding and using a pick in this book — that's beginner-level stuff that you can find in *Guitar For Dummies* (Wiley) — but I will point out that an alternative to using a pick is using your thumb, finger, or both. You can strum up and down across the strings with your bare thumb or index finger. Another option is to strum down with your thumb and up with your index finger. I demonstrate this technique in the second half of Video Clip 2.

An easy way to practice eighth-note picking and strumming techniques is to set your metronome for 100 BPM (give or take) and then alternate between eighth notes played with all downstrokes and eighth notes played by alternating the pickstrokes down, up, down, up, and so on. You can pick on any pitch or chord you like. When you get used to the moderate tempo of 100 BPM, try faster and slower tempos.

Exercising your eighths

Now that you know eighth notes and how to strum them, try working with an exercise that places eighth notes at various points in a measure. This helps you get a feel for mixing quarter notes and eighth notes, and prepares you to tackle the popular strum patterns later in this chapter.

As you play through Figure 3-4, you notice that no pick direction arrows are written above the rhythms for you as in previous examples. At this point, you should know to either use all downstrokes or alternate downstrokes and upstrokes. I recommend that you try both. You can hear my example in Audio Track 12. I play an open-A chord, but you can follow along with any form of A. You can also practice this exercise on your own using a metronome and any chord you like. When you get used to the 100 BPM tempo, try others.

Figure 3-4: Exercising your eighths.

© John Wiley & Sons, Inc.

Sustaining and Resting

As common as eighth notes are, so are eighth-note rests, which are periods of silence. And sometimes eighth notes are connected to each other with *ties,* which lengthens the duration of time that you sustain a note. Dotted quarter notes come into play here, too, because they have eighth notes added to their value. To make all these things work, guitarists use floating and damping techniques. In this section, I fill you in on all the details.

Fit to be tied

The ties that you get to know in Chapter 2 can be applied to eighth notes as well. Normally, you don't tie the first eighth note in an eighth-note pair to the second eighth note because that would make the pair the equivalent of a quarter note, in which case it's best to use a quarter note instead of a set of tied eighth notes. (Still with me?) Ties are used to sustain from the second eighth note in a set to the first eighth note in the next set, as shown in Figure 3-5. I demonstrate how to properly strum this figure in Video Clip 3.

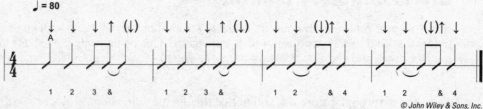

Figure 3-5: Playing eighth-note ties.

© John Wiley & Sons, Inc.

Floating over strings

Notice in the first two measures of Figure 3-5 that the "and" of beat three is tied to beat four. This means that the "and" of beat three is sustained through its normal eighth-note duration plus the duration of the quarter note on beat four. Because you sustain, you don't strike the strings on beat four.

Normally, beat four would be played with a downstroke. You still see the downward-pointing arrow above the beat, but it's put into parentheses to indicate that it isn't played.

Now, here's where things get hairy: Because you don't strike the strings on beat four, you may be inclined to cease the strumming motion of your picking hand, but don't do it! Instead, maintain your strumming motion and *skip over* the strings on beat four. Bypassing the strings in this manner is referred to as *floating, miming* (as in pantomime), or *phantom strumming* (or *phantom picking* when you play single-note lines). The technique enables you to keep your momentum and stay connected to the pulse. Its use becomes more critical as you progress to more complicated strum patterns.

Floating over the strings during sustained notes holds true for measures three and four as well, but in this case, beat two is sustained through to the first half of beat three, so you float on beat three and then strike the strings on the way up, the "and" of beat three.

Don't strike the strings when a note is tied to a note before it. To help illustrate this for now, I put parentheses around the sustained strokes.

Tick-tock

When it comes to guitar strumming and keeping perfect rhythm, the *tick-tock method* — constantly keeping your strumming hand in motion like a pendulum in a grand-father clock — is the way to go. In his song "Drivin' My Life Away," Eddie Rabbitt sings, "Those windshield wipers slappin' out a tempo, keepin' perfect rhythm with the song on the radio." That's another good way to think about the strumming movement — like that of windshield wipers.

In order to make it easy for you to work on playing ties, the tempo of Figure 3-5 is reduced to 80 BPM. Because you need to both hear the figure and see how the strumming motion resumes as ties are played and notes are sustained, watch the corresponding demonstration in Video Clip 3.

On the dot

Another way to notate a sustained note is with the use of a dot (see Chapter 2). A dot placed next to a note increases its length by half its value, so placing a dot after a quarter note (one beat) adds an eighth note (half a beat) to it. A dotted quarter note is worth one and a half beats. You see examples in Figure 3-6.

Figure 3-6: Playing dotted quarter notes.

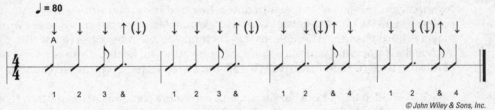

© John Wiley & Sons, Inc.

The rhythm is identical to Figure 3-5, only with dots instead of ties. The eighth note on beat three is held for only half a beat, so the dotted quarter note that follows comes in on the "and" of beat three and then sustains through all of beat four. The rhythm repeats in measure two. Measures three and four have dotted quarter notes on beat two, which means that you sustain into the first half of beat three and then strike the strings with an upstroke on the "and" of beat three before striking the strings on your way down on beat four.

From a rhythmic and strumming point of view, Figures 3-5 and 3-6 are identical. Go back and watch Video Clip 3.

The rest of the story

In addition to ties, eighth notes can also feature rests. An eighth-note rest looks like a fancy number seven. In Figure 3-7, you see the two places that eighth-note rests can be placed: either on or off the beat. In measure two, you play on the downstrokes and rest on the upstrokes. In measure four, you rest on the downstrokes and play on the upstrokes. To be sure you're resting right, play along with me in Video Clip 4.

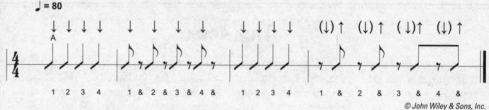

Figure 3-7:
Playing
eighth-note
rests.

© John Wiley & Sons, Inc.

Putting a damper on things

During periods of rest, you need to cut off the strings so that they're silent. Cutting off the sound of the strings is called *damping* or *choking* and is done in one of two ways:

- ✔ **Press your picking hand to the strings.** This works well when playing open-position chords.

- ✔ **Relax the pressure of your fretting-hand fingers.** This works well when playing barre chords.

You can see me demonstrate both damping techniques in Video Clip 4.

Playing Popular Patterns: Eighth Notes

Now that you're familiar with eighth notes, ties, and rests, you work with eighth-note strum patterns heard in popular music. With these examples, you play in various keys and begin playing chord changes. Throughout this section, you see references to specific songs that you can look up, learn, and play along with on your own. Each pattern is some combination of downstrokes (D) and upstrokes (U), as you see reflected in the figure captions.

Figure 3-8 (Video Clip 5) is a very basic and extremely common strum pattern that alternates between a downstroke and a downstroke/upstroke. You count it "1, 2 and, 3, 4 and" and strum it "down, down up, down, down up." To help you get started, arrows and counting are provided in the first measure. Repeat the same pattern of downstrokes and upstrokes from there.

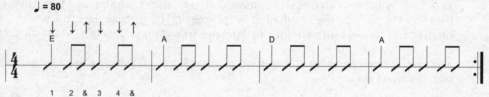

Figure 3-8:
Strum
pattern 1: D
DUD DU.

© John Wiley & Sons, Inc.

Variations of the basic Figure 3-8 feel, can be found in a variety of popular songs in various keys and at different tempos including, "Blowin' in the Wind" by Bob Dylan, "One of Us" by Joan Osborne, "You Were Meant for Me" by Jewel, "Patience" by Guns N' Roses, "Against the Wind" and "Night Moves" by Bob Seger, "Promises" and "Wonderful Tonight" by Eric Clapton, and "Ripple" by the Grateful Dead.

After you work out the pattern from the figure, look up the chord changes to some of the songs mentioned in the preceding paragraph and play along for practice.

Cheater, cheater, pumpkin eater

One problem that guitarists often run into is lack of time to move their fingers to the next chord in between changes. This is especially true when a measure ends with an upstroke and a new chord fingering is played on the very next downstroke (refer to Figures 3-8 and 3-9). At moderate and fast tempos, it's just not possible to hang onto a chord shape for the full measure and make the chord change in the next measure, so something has to give. In this case, you have to cheat by lifting your fingers off the strings early so that you can get a head start moving to the next chord. When you do this, you end up strumming open strings that may or may not be related to the chords and key, but they ring for only a split second and the end result is hardly noticeable.

You see an example of using a cheat stroke in the following figure. Notice that on the "and" of beat two, you see open strings in the tablature. These open strings are caused by your lifting your fingers off the E chord a little early and using the time to switch to A. The same thing happens as you transition from A to D, D to A, and A back to E. The necessity of the cheat stroke may not be apparent at the tempo of 80 BPM, but as you increase the tempo, it's easy to see how you simply have no choice but to use it. When you get this figure down, work with the same chord changes at increasingly faster tempos, and you'll see what I mean. Then play along with songs like "Gloria" by Van Morrison and "What I Like about You" by the Romantics, both of which use similar chord changes and cheat strokes. Many of the songs referenced with Figures 3-8 and 3-9 necessitate cheat strokes because of the upstroke at the end of the pattern. You see me demonstrate the technique in Video Clip 6.

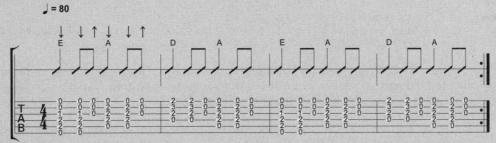

© John Wiley & Sons, Inc.

Whether cheat strokes are indicated in notation depends on the type of score. If it's one of those "note-for-note" transcriptions, you'll see every pitch sounded on the guitar, including those that are incidental, like cheat strokes. A score that is intended to give you just basic information, like a lead sheet, will not notate incidental pitches, even though they may be necessary in order to perform the music properly. Most guitar players don't give much thought to cheat strokes because the use of the technique comes naturally.

The songs I reference throughout this chapter don't always feature a particular strum pattern exactly as I teach it, but generally speaking, the feel of the pattern works with the music and something very similar is played in at least one song section.

As you begin with a new strum pattern, you may want to work with it on just one chord until you get a feel for the rhythm, and then move on to the full chord progression when you're ready.

Figure 3-8 can also be played using two chords per measure, with each chord held for only two beats. That's D DU change, D DU change, and so on as shown in Figure 3-9 and Video Clip 6. "I Got the Feelin'" by Neil Diamond uses the same pattern and chords.

Figure 3-9:
Two chords per measure.

© John Wiley & Sons, Inc.

Figure 3-10 (Video Clip 7) shows another strum pattern. It's two quarter notes followed by two sets of eighth notes. You count it "1, 2, 3 and, 4 and" and strum it "down, down, down up, down up" (or D D DUDU). In music, you see eighth notes connected in groups of either two or four. I opted to use beams across four eighth notes in measures three and four just to show what it looks like. Either way, you play the eighth notes the same way. I also wrote this one at 120 BPM so you can try your hand at a more lively tempo.

Figure 3-10:
Strum pattern 2: D D DUDU.

© John Wiley & Sons, Inc.

I mention "Drivin' My Life Away" by Eddie Rabbitt in the "Tick-tock" sidebar earlier in this chapter. It opens up with an E chord and this same strum pattern. Variations on this pattern are used in the key of D for Rod Stewart's "Maggie May."

The strum pattern in Figure 3-11 (Video Clip 8) has the "and" of beat two tied to beat three. This means that you don't strike the strings on beat three; instead, you sustain the chord from the previous strum and float over the strings with your picking hand on the way down. You then strike the strings with an upstroke on the "and" of three. You strum both beats one and four with downstrokes. All together, you count the rhythm "1, 2 and, and, 4" and strum it "down, down up, up, down" (or D DU U D).

Figure 3-11:
Strum pattern 3: D DU UD.

© John Wiley & Sons, Inc.

Van Morrison's "Brown-Eyed Girl" has the same chord changes and basic feel, though it's played at the much higher rate of 148 BPM, giving you something to work up to. Other songs on which you can use this strum pattern include "Stand by Me" by Ben E. King, "Sweet Child o' Mine" by Guns N' Roses, "Solitary Man" by Neil Diamond, "Under the Boardwalk" by the Drifters, "Man on the Moon" by R.E.M., and "Last Kiss" by Pearl Jam. "Patience" by Guns N' Roses, which features a bit of strum pattern 1 (refer to Figure 3-8), also has a section that uses strum pattern 2 (refer to Figure 3-10). Because Figure 3-11 is asymmetrical, it doesn't work to switch chords every two beats as you do with Figure 3-9.

When you get the feel of a pattern, you can use it together with any chords, in any key, in any combination, and at any tempo. My sample chord progressions are just examples to get you started. And there's no need to confine yourself to the open position — try moving up the neck with barre chords and other chord forms.

Next, in Figure 3-12, you work with hitting chords mostly on upstrokes. In fact, the only downstrokes used in this example occur on the first beat of each measure where the chord changes are placed. After starting each measure with a downstroke, it's all upstrokes for the remainder of it. Watch Video Clip 9 to see how it's done. Listen to Lynyrd Skynyrd's "Free Bird" beginning at the 4:43 mark for a similar use of this type of strumming.

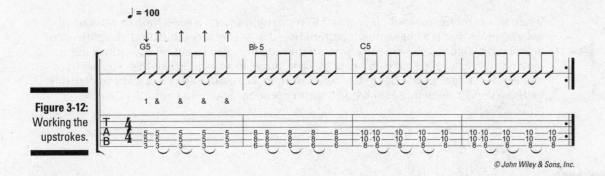

Figure 3-12: Working the upstrokes.

© John Wiley & Sons, Inc.

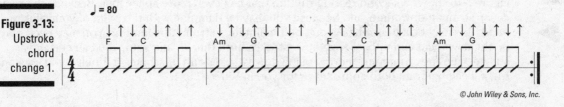

Figure 3-13: Upstroke chord change 1.

© John Wiley & Sons, Inc.

Figure 3-13 is an example that has a chord change on an upbeat and upstroke, specifically the "and" of beat two. Placing chord changes off the beat like this (or *offbeat*) seems to interrupt the regular flow of the rhythm and takes some getting used to. See Video Clip 10 for my demonstration.

Tom Petty's "Learning to Fly" uses the same chords and offbeat changes as Figure 3-13. Other songs that feature chord changes on the offbeat include "I Should Have Known Better" by The Beatles, "Mr. Jones" by Counting Crows, "Night Moves" and "You'll Accomp'ny Me" by Bob Seger, "Let It Rain" and "Layla" (from the album *Unplugged*) by Eric Clapton, and "Oye Como Va" by Santana.

When music has changes or accents that fall on something other than the most predictable beats, it is said to be *syncopated*.

Figure 3-14 has more upstroke changing action. In it, you play on the first two downbeats followed by the last two upbeats. If you maintain a steady down/up strumming motion, then the chord changes occur during upstrokes. You can also try the same rhythm without using the tick-tock motion, hitting everything with a downstroke instead. If you do, tap your foot and be sure to strike the strings on the appropriate downbeats and upbeats. I demonstrate both ways in Video Clip 11. Play this using power chords and some distortion, and it resembles "Living After Midnight" by Judas Priest.

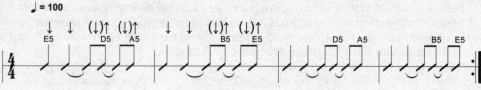

Figure 3-14: Upstroke chord change 2.

© John Wiley & Sons, Inc.

Resting Rhythms

While you're on the topic of playing eighth-note rhythms, it's a good time to work out a few examples that are not so much pattern based but more a combination of eighth notes and rests. In Figure 3-15, you see a rhythm that requires you to cut off the strings during moments of rest, specifically on beats two and three. In situations like this, you need to employ damping with one hand, the other, or both. I demonstrate a few ways to play this in Video Clip 12. Something similar is done in the song "Southern Cross" by Crosby, Stills & Nash.

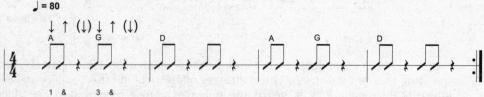

Figure 3-15: Resting rhythm 1.

© John Wiley & Sons, Inc.

Figure 3-16 shows a second resting rhythm that has even more space in it. Because the rests cause so much downtime, and because you may be damping with the palm of your picking hand, this may be a case where you don't maintain a strumming motion. You may even play on the downbeat and upbeat with downstrokes both times. That said, you can certainly still keep up the strumming motion using downstrokes and upstrokes if it helps you stay on track. I demonstrate both approaches for you in Video Clip 13.

Figure 3-16: Resting rhythm 2.

© John Wiley & Sons, Inc.

Counting this out, you play on beat one, rest on the "and" of one through to beat two, play on the "and" of two, and rest on beats three and four. This is when tapping your foot becomes a necessity. Keep track of the pulse and tap hard on all the downbeats: one, two, three, and four. Then strike the strings on beat one and the "and" of two (as your foot comes up). Everything else is silent. Because you strike the strings on an offbeat, this is an example of syncopation. "Don't Do Me Like That" by Tom Petty features a nearly identical rhythm guitar part.

Figure 3-17 is another example of a syncopated resting rhythm, this time with eighth notes played on the first two downbeats followed by the last two upbeats. It's a good idea to tap your foot here as well so you can keep track of the downbeats, especially in the second half of the measure so that you time the upbeat strokes properly. Be sure to cut off the strings during rests. Don't let beats one and two ring for more than an eighth note. That means that they should be cut off when your foot comes up. Likewise, you cut off the strings as your foot goes down in the second half of the measure. Every other measure has four full beats of rest.

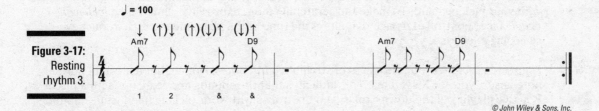

Figure 3-17: Resting rhythm 3.

You can maintain your strumming motion, which puts two strikes on downstrokes and two strikes on upstrokes, or use the stop-and-start method (or rather, the damp-and-strum method), striking the strings with downstrokes on both the downbeats and upbeats. I demonstrate both ways in Video Clip 14. You can use plain A-minor and D-major chord forms if it's easier for you. Santana's "Oye Como Va" is based on the same chord changes and a similar rhythm.

The resting and syncopation continues in Figure 3-18, this time with a simple rhythm that is repeated but displaced so that the hits land on downbeats the first time and on upbeats the second time. You strum on three downbeats in a row (one, two, and three), rest on beat 4, and then strum on three upbeats in a row (the "and" of four, the "and" of one, and the "and" of two). As you look at the notation, it's helpful to imagine each eighth note and rest as a regular pair of eighth notes connected by a beam; then take notice of whether to play on the first or second half of the pair. Every strike is sustained only the duration of an eighth note, and all space in between is silent. Notice the quarter-note rests on beats three and four of the second measure. As you count this out, it's "1, 2, 3, (4), and, and, and, (3, 4)." In addition to this tricky syncopation, you must change chords from F to E♭.

For this example, I recommend that you maintain your strumming motion, which puts three strikes on downstrokes and three strikes on upstrokes. You can see me play this way in Video Clip 15. "Tequila" by The Champs features the same chord changes and similar syncopation.

Figure 3-18: Resting rhythm 4.

Scratching the Surface

Earlier in this chapter, I give examples where chords are sustained and others where strings are cut off during periods of rest. Another technique that is common to rhythm guitar is the use of string scratching. This is where strings are cut off and damped, but instead of resting and floating over them, the strings are strummed, producing a scratching sound. Perhaps the most well-known example of string scratching among guitar players is Jimi Hendrix's "Voodoo Child (Slight Return)." The song opens up with percussive-like scratches that are sounded simply by damping the strings with your fretting hand and strumming across them with your picking hand. To make the scratching more expressive, Jimi used a *wah-wah pedal,* a foot-controlled device that alters the tone of the instrument with a frequency-sweeping effect.

Figure 3-19 includes four measures of straight eighth notes. Notice that instead of normal note heads, you see X symbols. This indicates that the sounds are dead, not actual pitches. Practice playing all the downstrokes and upstrokes with your picking hand while damping the strings with your fretting hand. To see how this is done, watch Video Clip 16.

When you damp the strings, apply only enough pressure to prevent them from ringing. Don't push the strings down to the fretboard so as to sound pitches.

Figure 3-19:
String scratching 1.

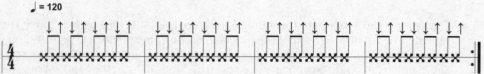

© John Wiley & Sons, Inc.

Figure 3-20 is an exercise to set you up for the figure that follows it. It also prepares you for some of the rhythms you encounter in Chapter 4. It features a very popular type of syncopation that can be a challenge to read in notation, but easy to get the feel for. It's a pattern that alternates nonconsecutive downstrokes and upstrokes. All together, and keeping a steady down/up motion, it's down, scratch scratch, up, scratch scratch, down, scratch scratch, up, scratch scratch, and so on. Rather than try to count this out, I suggest that you look away from the notation example and work out the alternating pattern on your own, continuing it until you play it by feel. Watch my example in Video Clip 17.

Figure 3-20:
String scratching 2.

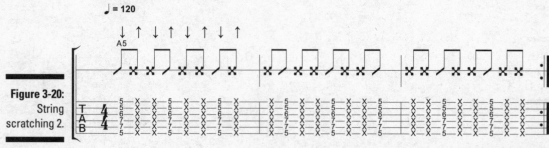

© John Wiley & Sons, Inc.

The next example, Figure 3-21, mixes chords with scratched strokes. I added tablature to this example so that you can follow along playing in the very same position as I do in Video Clip 18. You need to lift your fingers off the E5 chord and reach across the strings during the scratched strokes, moving quickly to get your fingers back in place for the next chord. Before you try to tackle the whole figure, try playing and repeating only measures one and two. When you're ready, move onto measure three.

Measure three features a bit of the alternating pattern from the previous figure and measure four has a new rhythm for you to work out. "China Grove" by The Doobie Brothers follows the same overall rhythm as Figure 3-21, using some of the same chords.

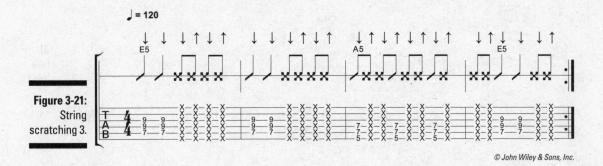

Figure 3-21: String scratching 3.

© John Wiley & Sons, Inc.

The example in Figure 3-22 has far less scratching but may be more challenging to play because it's tricky to fit in only one quick scratch while sustaining the chords the rest of the time. Notice that the chord changes happen on the upstrokes, the "and" of four in each measure (except in the last measure, but you're welcome to do an early switch back to C#m on the repeat too). The style here is reminiscent of "Sister Golden Hair" by America. You see me play it in Video Clip 19.

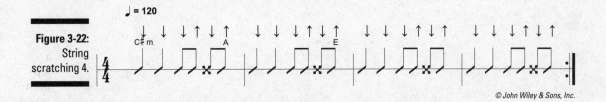

Figure 3-22: String scratching 4.

© John Wiley & Sons, Inc.

Chapter 4

Playing Sixteenth-Note Strum Patterns

*I*n this chapter, you move on from the previous chapter's eighth-note strum patterns and get busy with sixteenth notes. You continue to work with ties, dots, rests, damping, floating, and scratching, plus play specific patterns that are common to popular music. I break down those clean, tight, funky rhythms that may give you trouble into easy-to-follow steps. Finally, I help you add a new technique, accenting, to your strumming repertoire.

Sweet Sixteenths

In Chapter 2, you work with quarter notes, which are notes played on every beat in common time, 4/4. In Chapter 3, you split each beat in half, creating eighth notes. Now you split eighth notes in half to create sixteenth notes.

In Figure 4-1 (Video Clip 20), you see sixteenth notes in context, by note values progressing from quarters to eighths to sixteenths. An eighth note looks like a quarter note with an added flag on its stem. The sixteenth note adds an additional flag for a total of two. Like eighth notes, sixteenth notes can be written individually or connected in groups of two and four with the use of beams.

In Figure 4-1, I use downstrokes and upstrokes on the eighth notes in measure two. As you play through the example, you double the rate of your strumming when you get to the sixteenth notes. You can also play eighth notes by doubling up on the downstrokes. When you play eighth notes with all downstrokes, you only need to strike the strings on the way up to fill in with sixteenths.

In addition to playing Figure 4-1 as written, take some time on your own to practice alternating between measures of eighth and sixteenth notes.

Like quarter and eighth notes, sixteenth notes are counted so as to identify all sixteen points in a measure. Quarter notes are counted "1, 2, 3, 4." Eighth notes subdivide the beats by adding *and*s between the quarter notes and are counted "1 and 2 and 3 and 4 and" (with the ampersand [&] sign often used to save space). Sixteenth notes subdivide once more, adding two more points in between each eighth note. The point in between a beat and its *and* is called "e" (long E, as in *meet*). The point in between the *and* and the next beat is called "a" (as in *uh*). All together, sixteenth notes are counted "1 e and a, 2 e and a, 3 e and a, 4 e and a" (often written 1 e & a, 2 e & a, . . .).

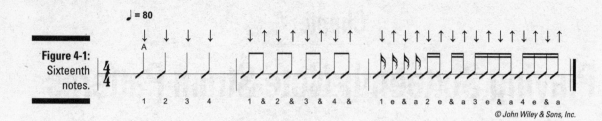

Figure 4-1:
Sixteenth
notes.

© John Wiley & Sons, Inc.

Throughout this chapter, you mainly work on rhythm examples that feature ties, dots, rests, and scratches, creating popular patterns that float over the strings at some point. Before you get to these patterns, though, play through Figure 4-2, an example of playing on every single downstroke and upstroke. Arrows and counting are provided in the first measure only. You repeat the same strumming and rhythm in the second measure. Be sure to take notice of the chords used, which are written just above the notes and below the arrows. They change from the first to second measure. You can hear me play through Figure 4-2 in Audio Track 13.

Steve Miller Band's "Take the Money and Run" is played in a very similar manner as Figure 4-2, hitting on every sixteenth-note beat with a fair amount of consistency, though it may take you some time to work up to its 96 BPM tempo. "Get Down Tonight" by KC and the Sunshine Band, played all the way up at 116 BPM, features the chord changes F7sus4-F7 (and later, Cm-B♭) played with a constant sixteenth-note strumming motion through the entire song. It's quite a workout!

Use the extra click at the end of all the audio tracks to practice on your own.

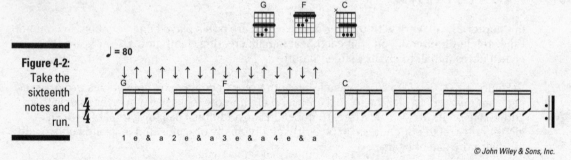

Figure 4-2:
Take the
sixteenth
notes and
run.

© John Wiley & Sons, Inc.

Popular Patterns: Sixteenth Notes

The first actual pattern you work with is nearly all sixteenths, with the exception of two eighth notes on beats one and three. Notice that the very first stem in Figure 4-3 has one beam, while the two sixteenth notes that follow it have two beams. This means that the first time you strike the strings, you hold for the duration of an eighth note, both 1 and "e" when you count sixteenths. The pair of sixteenth notes that follow are "and a," and complete the first beat in the measure. The second beat is all sixteenths, "2 e and a." The same thing happens with beats three and four. All together, you count each measure, "1 and a, 2 e and a, 3 and a, 4 e and a." This means that your picking hand is strumming down down up, down up down up, down down up, down up down up" ("D DUDUDU D DUDUDU"). Watch me do it in Video Clip 21.

Keep your hand in constant motion and float over the strings with an upstroke on the "e" of beats one and three.

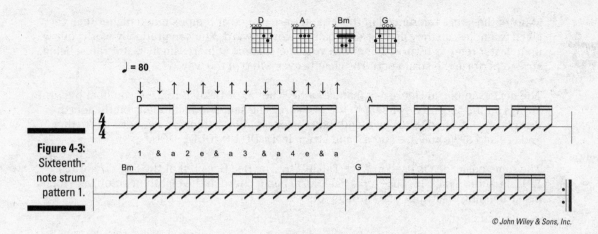

Figure 4-3:
Sixteenth-note strum pattern 1.

© John Wiley & Sons, Inc.

The very same strum pattern is used at 98 BPM in the song "Hey, Soul Sister" by Train, even using the same kind of chord changes, though you need to place a capo at the second fret of your guitar and play the chord shapes two frets higher in order to match the recording.

In Chapter 3, you get started with the *cheat stroke,* which is the technique of lifting your fingers off a chord early in order to move to the next chord in time. You may need to play the last upstroke before each chord change in Figure 4-3 as open strings so that you can have your fingers in place by the next chord and downstroke. Another trick is to start each new chord by first only fretting and picking its root, giving yourself an extra split second to form the rest of the chord shape and continue with full strumming. For example, when switching to the A chord from D, pick down on the root, A (the open fifth string if you're using open-position chords), first; then get your fingers in place for the full chord shape and resume full strumming. From A to Bm, you can fret and pick the B at the second fret first, and then finish building the rest of the chord shape and resume full strumming. Same thing on the G chord: Reach for and play the root, G, at the third fret of the sixth string first.

The example in Figure 4-4 combines eighth and sixteenth notes as well, taking the same rhythm from the previous figure on beat one and simply repeating it on all beats. The result is that you float over the strings on every "e" after each beat. You count it "1 and a, 2 and a, 3 and a, 4 and a" and strum it "D DUD DUD DUD DU."

You can hear me demonstrate this in Audio Track 14 using an E5 power chord in the open position. The galloping effect that this pattern makes is reminiscent of Heart's "Barracuda" when played at 130 BPM (a tempo you should slowly work up to).

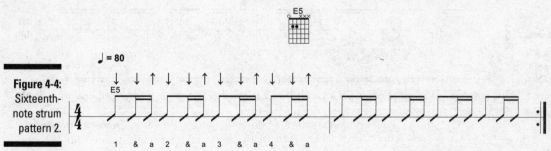

Figure 4-4:
Sixteenth-note strum pattern 2.

© John Wiley & Sons, Inc.

Many of the songs referenced in this chapter are played at tempos much higher than the given examples, so they make great goals to work toward. You can gradually work your way up to faster tempos by practicing with your metronome at increasingly faster rates, being sure to perform the strum patterns cleanly every step of the way.

The next example, in Figure 4-5, features a tie. The "a" of 1 is tied to 2, so you float over the strings on the second downbeat in the measure. The same thing happens on the fourth downbeat — it's tied to the sixteenth note before it. All together, you count this rhythm "1 e and a, e and a, 3 e and a, e and a," and strum it "DUDU UDUDUDU UDU."

The same basic idea is used in "Jive Talkin'" by The Bee Gees but at the fast rate of 104 BPM. In Audio Track 15, I use a partial E form barre chord in the eighth position, and focus my strumming on strings one through four.

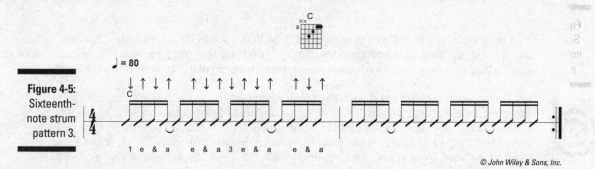

Figure 4-5:
Sixteenth-
note strum
pattern 3.

© John Wiley & Sons, Inc.

Figure 4-6 is a combination of the previous two examples. You play an eighth and two sixteenths on beats one and two, followed by sixteenth notes with a tie from the "a" of beat three to beat four. The measure is counted "1 and a, 2 and a, 3 e and a, e and a" and strummed "D DUD DUDUDU UDU."

The feel of this pattern works well at 96 BPM in "6th Avenue Heartache" by The Wallflowers, though you need a capo at the third fret to match the pitch of the recording. I demonstrate Figure 4-6 for you in Audio Track 16.

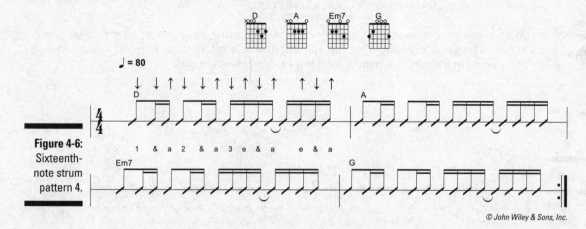

Figure 4-6:
Sixteenth-
note strum
pattern 4.

© John Wiley & Sons, Inc.

Figure 4-7 is an example of an eighth-note-based strum pattern that features periodic sixteenths. Basically, you strum eighth notes the whole time and only use a quick pair of sixteenth notes just before the chord changes. The eighth notes are played with downstrokes in the example so that your strumming rate is on pace to switch to sixteenths with a quick upstroke. You can use a regular F chord in place of the Fsus2 if need be.

You can hear me demonstrate this style of strumming on Audio Track 17. Something similar is done in "I Melt with You" by Modern English, though at the much higher rate of 154 BPM.

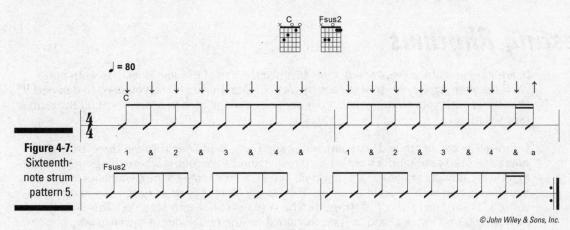

Figure 4-7: Sixteenth-note strum pattern 5.

© John Wiley & Sons, Inc.

For the next example, in Figure 4-8, you play a mixture of eighth and sixteenth notes with a chord change in an unusual location. The rhythm is counted "1 and, 2 and a, 3 e and, 4 and" and strummed "D D D DUDUD D D." The chord change to G, occurs on the "e" of beat three, which is the last upstroke in the group of four sixteenth notes that begin on the "and" of beat two. After beginning the second measure with Dsus4, the A7sus4 chord also lands on the "e" of beat three and is played using an upstroke. Aside from the sixteenth notes in between beats 2 and 3, everything else is eighth notes.

You can hear me play this example in Audio Track 18. If you work your way up from 65 BPM to 87 BPM over time, then you can play along with "Wonderwall" by Oasis.

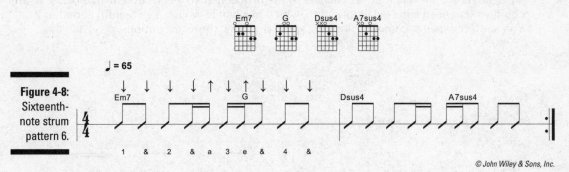

Figure 4-8: Sixteenth-note strum pattern 6.

© John Wiley & Sons, Inc.

With guitar strumming and chord changing, it's easy to coordinate your hands and make a chord change when the change occurs on a predictable beat and downstroke. What makes some patterns tricky is when the switching occurs on an unpredictable beat or with an upstroke, both of which happen in Figure 4-8. You would expect the G and A7sus4 chords to begin on beats three with downstrokes, not the sixteenth notes and upstrokes that follow. Nevertheless, it's fairly common for guitarists to use patterns like this, so you need to get a feel for them. It helps to start slowly. I set the tempo in Figure 4-8 at 65 BPM for this reason.

TIP

It's a good idea to work out and practice some rhythms on just one chord before trying to follow the chord changes. A strum pattern like Figure 4-8 can be played in its entirety using only the first chord, Em7. When you get a feel for the pattern itself, you can work toward adding in the chord changes. Taking things one step at a time like this holds true for all rhythm examples in this chapter.

Resting Rhythms

In addition to featuring sustained notes through the use of ties and dots, sixteenth-note rhythms often have periods of silence by way of rests. During rests, you need to dampen the strings with your fretting hand, your picking hand, or both in order to cut off the strings (see Chapter 3).

Figure 4-9 mixes eighth and sixteenth notes and rests. Beats one through three are eighth notes and pretty straightforward, "1 and, rest, 3 and." Beat four is where things get interesting. On the downbeat of four is a new type of rest, a *sixteenth-note rest,* which looks like an eighth-note rest with an additional flag. Thinking of all four parts of beat 4 (4 e and a), you rest on "4" and then strike the strings on the very next sixteenth note, "e." This sixteenth note is then tied to "and" and "a" and sustained for the remainder of the measure.

PLAY THIS!

You can hear me play through this example in Audio Track 19. Whether to maintain a constant strumming motion and play the "e" of "4" with an upstroke (as written), or tap your foot and punch out the rhythm all with downstrokes is your call. I suggest trying it both ways. This rhythm, when combined with power chords and distortion at 96 BPM, is reminiscent of "I Love Rock and Roll" by Joan Jett and The Blackhearts.

There are four measures in Figure 4-9 and they all use the very same rhythm. However, each measure looks different at the end. In the first measure, you see single sixteenth notes tied together. In the second measure, the same sixteenth notes are connected with a beam. In the third measure, the last two sixteenth notes have been combined into one eighth note, which is simply another way to write the same rhythm. Measure four also ends with an eighth note, but this time it connects to the proceeded sixteenth note with a beam. I could've also used a dotted eighth note, which has half its value, a sixteenth, added to it. You see that when it comes to notating some rhythms, there are options.

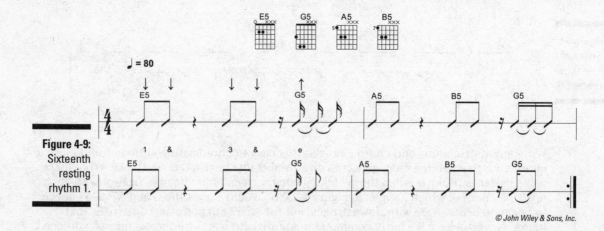

Figure 4-9:
Sixteenth resting rhythm 1.

Figure 4-10 features sixteenth notes, a sixteenth-note rest, plus eighth notes and a half note. The best way to work out this rhythm is to first play it as if the rest weren't there and the first beat included four sixteenth notes in a row. When viewed like this, you count it "1 e and a, 2 and, 3" and strum it "DUDUD D D" Next, bypass the second downstroke on the "and" of 1 and you got it as written. When played properly you count it "1 e a, 2 and, 3" and strum it "DU UD D D"

Work your way up to 96 BPM and this rhythm and two major seven chords sound like the first part of the "These Eyes" chorus by Guess Who. I demonstrate the figure for you in Audio Track 20.

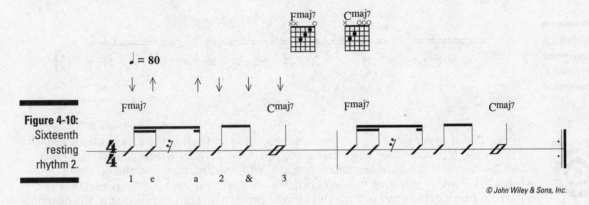

Figure 4-10: Sixteenth resting rhythm 2.

© John Wiley & Sons, Inc.

Scratching

A technique common to rhythm guitar is scratching, where strings are damped and strummed producing a scratching sound. Figure 4-11 (Audio Track 21) is an example of using this technique along with sixteenth and eighth notes. You keep a steady sixteenth-note motion through the whole figure, using downstrokes to play the chords on "1 and" and "3 and." In between each chord, you relax your fretting hand, damp the strings, and strum a group of sixteenth-note scratches. Put it all together and you count it "1 and, 2 e and a, 3 and, 4 e and a" and strum it "D D DUDUD D DUDU." You hear this technique used in Led Zeppelin's "Stairway to Heaven" during the song's final verse, played at about 100 BPM.

The next scratching example, in Figure 4-12, features an alternating pattern similar to Figure 3-19 in Chapter 3, only this time using sixteenth notes. The pattern is "chord scratch scratch, chord scratch scratch, chord scratch scratch, chord scratch scratch." Because the rhythm is set to sixteenth notes, the first F chord is sounded with a downstroke on beat 1, the next F chord with an upstroke on the "a" of beat one, followed by another downstroke on the "and" of beat two, then another upstroke on the "e" of beat three.

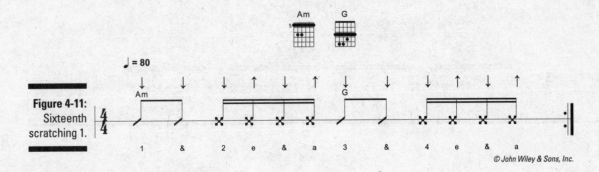

Figure 4-11: Sixteenth scratching 1.

© John Wiley & Sons, Inc.

Beat four of Figure 4-12 is pretty straightforward. Strike an F chord on beat four, strike a G chord on the "and" of beat four, and put two damped strokes in between. Follow along with me in Audio Track 22. This rhythm is also featured in "Stairway to Heaven." Put it together with the Figure 4-11, and you see what I mean.

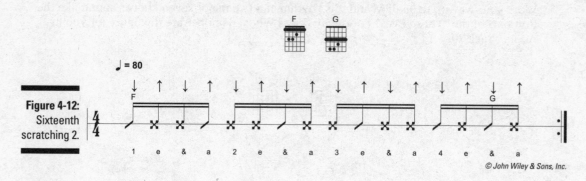

Figure 4-12: Sixteenth scratching 2.

© John Wiley & Sons, Inc.

You may find it easier to disregard the actual counting and instead just think about sounding the chord on every other downstroke and upstroke. In other words, sound the chord on nonconsecutive downstrokes and upstrokes. When you do this, you end up with two strokes in between each strike of the chord. It's on these two strokes in between that you relax your fretting hand and scratch the strings. Before you read any further in the notation, I recommend you work with this concept I just outlined, repeating it on an F chord until it becomes second nature.

You don't know diddly

In *Rock Guitar For Dummies* (Wiley), Jon Chappell writes, "One of the biggest influences in bringing the R&B sound to rock guitar was Bo Diddley. One of Diddley's best-known songs was an anthem he composed for himself, he named after himself, and that used a syncopated rhythm that became synonymous with his name. He immortalized the 'Bo Diddley beat' and was copied by everyone from Buddy Holly to the Rolling Stones."

The following figure, which you can hear in Audio Track 23, is a rhythm-guitar passage that employs

the so-called "Bo Diddley beat." You can play it by hitting only the specific downstrokes and upstrokes indicated above the slash notation, or use continuous strumming with dampening and scratching as seen in the tablature. Variations on this strum pattern can be heard on the songs "Willie and the Hand Jive" by Johnny Otis, "Not Fade Away" by Buddy Holly, and "Faith" by George Michael.

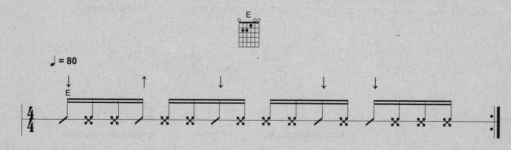

Four Steps to Funky

One of the hardest things for guitar players to get a feel for is funky sixteenth-note rhythms with lots of syncopation and rests. In this section, you take a look at a rhythm in four ways and train yourself to play one aspect of it in each example until you put it all together for a final product that sounds straight out of a '70s funk tune. Stay with me here, because it doesn't sound too funky right out of the gate, but its groove increases with each step. Also, you learn this a little differently than you do the previous examples in this chapter.

In the first step, Figure 4-13, I introduce the pattern — that is, on which downstrokes and upstrokes you strike the chord. This rhythm is set to sixteenth notes, and you see them in the staff, but the actual pattern is not notated. Instead, look at the down and up arrows above the staff and work out the pattern from there. The strokes in parentheses are to float over the strings, allowing the chord to sustain. The strokes not in parentheses make up the pattern that you build on in this section, so make sure to hit them accurately and strongly. I also indicate below the staff each part of the beat that you hit, but honestly, this rhythm is so sparse that it doesn't help much to see this information. Instead, you really need to learn this by rote and rehearse until it becomes second nature. Listening to my example in Audio Track 24 will help.

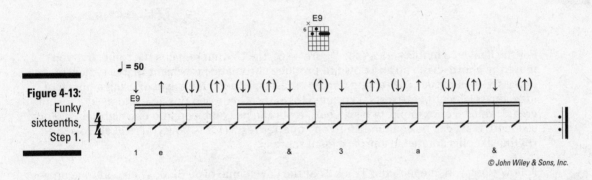

Figure 4-13: Funky sixteenths, Step 1.

© John Wiley & Sons, Inc.

In the next step (see Figure 4-14), you add scratches. All the strokes in parentheses from the previous example are now played, but you relax your fretting hand so as to damp the strings and produce the scratching sound. When you play this correctly, your picking hand steadily strums and your fretting hand only puts pressure on the strings when the chord should sound. It's almost as if your fretting hand is in control of the pattern, squeezing the guitar neck at just the right time to sound the chord. Notice that the tempo is increased to 60 BPM. Follow along with me in Audio Track 25.

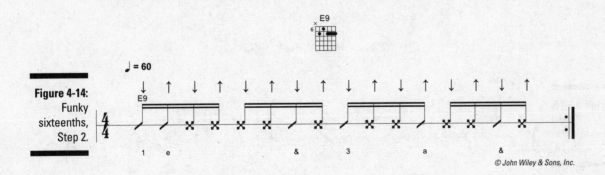

Figure 4-14: Funky sixteenths, Step 2.

© John Wiley & Sons, Inc.

Moving along to Figure 4-15, the main rhythm hasn't changed, but all the scratches from the previous example are now played as rests, which means that you need to both dampen the strings with your fretting hand and float over the strings with your picking hand. This is what I meant by "sparse" earlier — there's a lot of empty space. Both measures in the figure feature the same rhythm, but I use single sixteenth notes in measure one and beams in measure two, just to show you the different ways that rhythms like this can be notated. All the rests are written as sixteenth-note rests with each one representing one rested (or floated) sixteenth-note stroke. The tempo has been increased again to 70 BPM, working its way up to a more lively pace. Follow along with me in Audio Track 26 and then continue to work with this exercise until it's second nature to you.

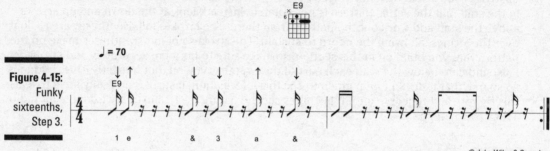

Figure 4-15:
Funky
sixteenths,
Step 3.

For the final step in this series (see Figure 4-16), the rhythm remains the same, but you move the chord shape up and down to produce chromatic movement that is typical of funky styles of music. The resting remains the same, too, but instead of using a bunch of individual sixteenth-note rests, I grouped them together when possible and used a rest of greater value. For example, two sixteenth rests can be combined into one eighth rest. Four sixteenth rests can be combined into one quarter rest. This is how you're likely to see a rhythm like this notated in a professional score.

Follow along with me in Audio Track 27 at the new tempo of 80 BPM. Then continue on your own until the rhythm and chord movement are both second nature to you.

To play the E♭9 you simply slide the very same E9 shape down one fret and strike it with a downstroke on the "and" of beat two. You return to E9 on beat three. To play the F♯9, you slide the shape up two frets and strike it with an upstroke on the "a" of beat three. Then you slide down one fret to F9 and strike it with a downstroke on the "and" of beat four. You return to E9 at the top of the next measure. Again, the rhythm hasn't changed from the previous three figures, and your strumming hand is not doing anything differently. Only your fretting hand changes by moving the ninth chord around.

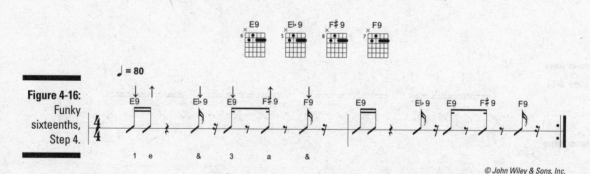

Figure 4-16:
Funky
sixteenths,
Step 4.

Don't try to rush through Figure 4-16. Instead, work through it slowly and in segments, giving yourself time to get used to the placement of each chord.

If you can work your way up to 110 BPM, you can play along with "Play That Funky Music" by Wild Cherry, which features a very similar guitar part that uses techniques found in all three steps in this section: sustaining, scratching, and resting.

When you master each step in this section individually, you can borrow a little from each example to give the final part some variation. In other words, you can sustain some chords instead of always cutting them off. You can scratch strings in place of some of the rests. Perhaps you add additional rests. Eventually, you may even change up the rhythm itself, striking the chords on some of the other downstrokes and upstrokes. When you play funky guitar rhythms, allow the groove of the music and your personal feel guide you.

Accenting the Positive

One final strumming technique and notation marking to cover before wrapping up this chapter is accents. *Accents* are cues to strum a particular part of the beat harder to give it more emphasis. In Figure 4-17, you see two measures of sixteenth notes, which you strum with constant alternating downstrokes and upstrokes, but some beats have an accent symbol (>) just above them indicating that they should be played with more emphasis. It helps to strum a little lighter in between the accents in order to make the accents themselves more apparent. The pattern, which accents nonconsecutive downstrokes and upstrokes in an alternating fashion and then finishes with two downstrokes at the end, is used in Figure 4-12. Whereas Figure 4-12 uses scratching in between the main chord hits, Figure 4-17 maintains light strumming and uses accents.

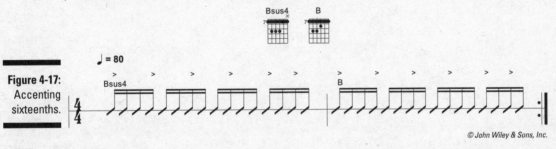

Figure 4-17: Accenting sixteenths.

© John Wiley & Sons, Inc.

Listen to me demonstrate Figure 4-17 in Audio Track 28. When you work your way up to 132 BPM, the chords and accent pattern sound like The Who's "Pinball Wizard."

Many of the examples in this chapter can be played with accents for a slightly different sound and feel. Instead of playing any ties, dots, rests, or scratches, just play through each figure using constant downstrokes and upstrokes; then accent the proper beats to outline the pattern. Remember to keep the strumming in between soft so that the harder-strummed accents stick out and define the rhythm. Accents are used with all types of note values, including eighths. The eighth-note examples in Chapter 3 can be played in an accented style, too. Try it!

Chapter 5

Playing Triplets, Shuffles, and Compound Time Signatures

In This Chapter

▶ Getting to know triplets

▶ Playing shuffles

▶ Working with compound time signatures

▶ Access the audio tracks and video clips at www.dummies.com/go/guitarrhythmtechnique

In Chapters 2, 3, and 4, you subdivide note values into even parts like halves, quarters, eighths, and sixteenths, and work with time signatures based on quarter notes. In this chapter, you take a look at how a beat can be divided into three parts called a *triplet,* and work with time-signature examples that are based on eighth notes. Plus, you get to know the *shuffle,* which is a type of groove common to many styles of popular music.

Three-Ring Circus: Playing Triplets

When you divide a quarter-note beat into two equal parts, it's called an eighth note. When you divide a beat into three equal parts, it's called an *eighth-note triplet.* A triplet is considered an irregular rhythm because its metric value is an odd number, as opposed to regular rhythms like eighths and sixteenths, which subdivide evenly. Playing triplets is a little tricky at first because it feels as though the music has changed tempos and/or time signatures, but when you get a sense of the triplet's oddness (pun intended), you find that the irregular rhythm is actually a regular player in music.

You see triplets used in Figure 5-1. Like eighth notes, they have flags and are connected with beams, but triplets will always have a number 3 above them and often a bracket as well. To hear exactly how these triplets should be played, listen to Audio Track 29.

Triplets are counted in one of three ways:

▶ **Use the two syllables in the word *triplet* together with the beat number.** For example, "1 trip-let, 2 trip-let, 3 trip-let, 4 trip-let." In the case of Figure 5-1, you count it "1, 2, 3, 4 trip-let."

▶ **Count 1 and a.** Figure 5-1 can also be counted "1, 2, 3, 4 and a" or "1, 2, 3, 4 & a."

▶ **Simply use 123.** So Figure 5-1 can also be counted "1, 2, 3, 123."

Figure 5-1:
Triplet
example 1.

© John Wiley & Sons, Inc.

Transitioning from quarter notes to eighth-note triplets is not simply a matter of doubling your rate; it's a matter of increasing your rate from one that is even-based to one that is odd-based. As a result, there isn't always a way to neatly arrange the downstrokes and upstrokes you use while strumming. When you get to the triplet group at the end of each measure in Figure 5-1, you strum it either "DUD" or "DDD." You can try it both ways for now.

Notice that when you strum "DUD," you need to make an adjustment when you begin the next measure, a quick change back to a downstroke. Another option is to play beat one of the next measure with an upstroke, and then get yourself turned around straight to play beat two with a downstroke.

Perhaps the most universally recognizable example of using triplets is heard in the main theme to *Star Wars*. Tap it out right now from memory, and you'll see what I mean. Triplets are also featured in the 20th Century Fox fanfare you hear at the beginning of many films.

Next, in Figure 5-2, you play triplet eighth notes on every beat. Because you strum at a steady rate throughout, in this case, you can consistently alternate between downstrokes and upstrokes without needing to make any adjustments. You see down and up arrows above the staff in the example. The only thing that may seem unusual to you is striking downbeats two and four with upstrokes. You also have the option of playing all of Figure 5-2 with downstrokes. I demonstrate the figure in Audio Track 30.

Figure 5-2:
Triplet
example 2.

© John Wiley & Sons, Inc.

It's very rare to strum constant triplets like you see in Figure 5-2. The only example that comes to mind is "All My Loving" by The Beatles. It features a rhythm guitar that strums through the chord changes using constant triplets at the rather fast rate of 154 BPM.

Figure 5-3 introduces you to the triplet eighth-note rest, which looks like a regular eighth-note rest, but like its eighth-note counterpart, is set apart through the use of a triplet bracket. When you get to the triplet sets, you play only the first two triplet beats, and then rest on the third one. Beginning with beat three in the second measure, you count it "3 trip (let), 4 trip (let)," with a rest on each "let" (hence, the parentheses). In this example, it works well to use all downstrokes and dampen the strings with the side of your picking hand during rests. Play along in Audio Track 31. Add some distortion to sound like "For Whom the Bell Tolls" by Metallica. The same song also features a second guitar that plays a melodic motif set to triplets.

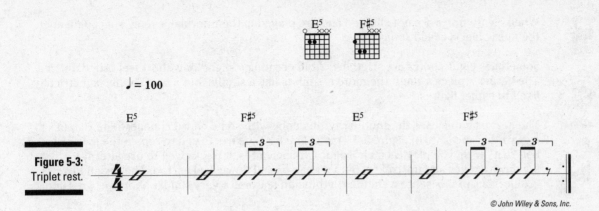

Figure 5-3:
Triplet rest.

© John Wiley & Sons, Inc.

Next, in Figure 5-4 (Audio Track 32), you see an example of tied triplets. Here, the first two parts of each triplet are tied together, giving you alternating long and short notes. You can strum either with downstrokes and upstrokes as I've notated, or with all downstrokes. When this bouncy feel is constant in a piece of music, it's given a special name and notated in a manner that you get to know in the next section.

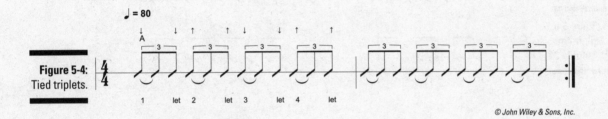

Figure 5-4:
Tied triplets.

© John Wiley & Sons, Inc.

Lost in the Shuffle

When music has a constant tied-triplet feel with long and short notes like Figure 5-4, it's called a *shuffle* or, more specifically, an *eighth-note shuffle*. In this case, rather than notate the music with continuous triplets and ties, the score is simplified by using plain eighth notes, but with a special performance note that instructs you to play them all in a long/short shuffle manner.

Take a look at Figure 5-5. It appears to be plain eighth notes, but the little equation at the top left instructs you to play each pair of eighth notes as if they were a triplet with the first two parts combined into one longer note (two eighth-note triplets combined to make a quarter note). This makes the notation less congested and easier to read. You can even count the eighth notes in a normal manner, "1 and, 2 and, 3 and, 4 and"; just keep in mind that they're always played with a shuffle feel. When you play Figure 5-5 correctly, it sounds the same as Figure 5-4 and Audio Track 32.

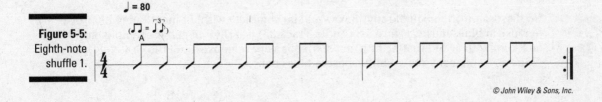

Figure 5-5:
Eighth-note
shuffle 1.

© John Wiley & Sons, Inc.

When eighth notes are not shuffled and are played in their normal, evenly spaced manner, the music feel is called *straight time*.

Sometimes eighth notes are stretched a bit, creating a slight long/short feel called a *swing*. The harder a piece swings, the more it sounds like a shuffle, but a true shuffle is metrically fixed to triplet figures.

The next example uses the shuffle rhythm along with some chord changes. The sign in every other measure of Figure 5-6 (Audio Track 33) instructs you to repeat the measure before it. In all, you play each chord for two measures. It works well to use alternating downstrokes and upstrokes, but you can use all downstrokes, too. The Beach Boys' "California Girls" is set to a shuffle rhythm and features a very similar chord progression.

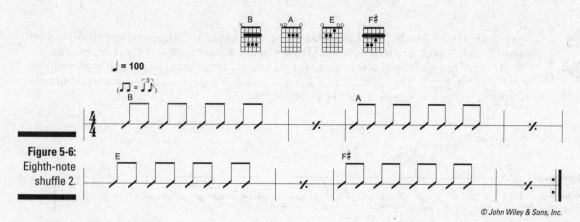

Figure 5-6:
Eighth-note
shuffle 2.

© John Wiley & Sons, Inc.

Next, in Figure 5-7, you see a chord progression set to a shuffle rhythm that mixes quarter notes and tied eighth notes. You count it "1, 2 and, and, 4" and strum it "D DU UD," but with a shuffle feel the whole time. This pattern is identical to Figure 3-10 back in Chapter 3, but here it's played with a shuffle feel rather than in straight time. You can hear me demonstrate the shuffle time in Audio Track 34. "All My Loving" by The Beatles features multiple guitar tracks, including one following the same pattern with similar chord changes, but at the rate of 154 BPM.

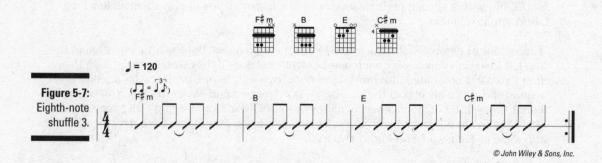

Figure 5-7:
Eighth-note
shuffle 3.

© John Wiley & Sons, Inc.

No discussion about shuffle rhythms would be complete without mentioning its prevalent use in blues music. Figure 5-8 (Audio Track 35) is a rhythm guitar example based on an E root with an alternating fifth and sixth. It's very reminiscent of the Grateful Dead's "Truckin'" and many other shuffle-based, blues songs.

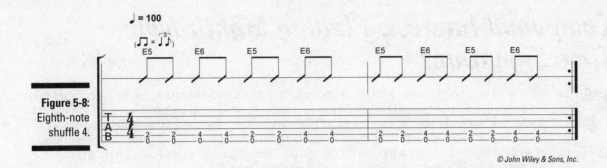

Figure 5-8:
Eighth-note shuffle 4.

© John Wiley & Sons, Inc.

Shuffles are fairly common in popular music. A few more examples include "Hound Dog" by Elvis Presley, "Think It Over" by Buddy Holly, "Don't Stop" by Fleetwood Mac, "Fool in the Rain" by Led Zeppelin, "Hide Away" by Freddie King, "Cold Shot" by Stevie Ray Vaughan, and "Roadhouse Blues" by The Doors.

It's possible to play a sixteenth-note shuffle as well. In this case, each eighth note is split into three. In the same way that you can think of regular sixteenths as being twice the rate of eighths, you can think of a sixteenth-note shuffle as an eighth-note shuffle at twice the rate, playing the sixteenths with the same kind of lilting feel that shuffled eighths have. A few examples include Toto's "Rosanna" and Bob Marley's "Stir It Up."

Triplet quarter note

Another way that groups of three can be used is in the form of a triplet quarter note. This is when you split a half note into three parts. You can also think of it as playing three notes in the span of time normally taken up by two. You can see examples in the following figure. Listen to Audio Track 36 to be sure you're playing the quarter-note triplet correctly.

You hear quarter-note triplets in the final refrain of Buddy Holly's "That'll Be the Day." The Beatles were big on the quarter-note triplet. You hear its use in the bridge of "We Can Work It Out" when they sing, "fussing and fighting my friend," the opening guitar in "Ticket to Ride," the chorus piano riff in "Drive My Car," and the chorus in "Magical Mystery Tour" when they sing, "going to take you away."

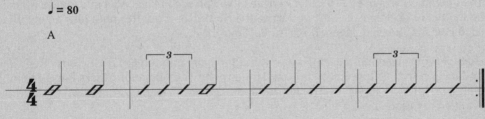

© John Wiley & Sons, Inc.

Compound Interest: Playing Eighth-Note Time Signatures

Instead of notating shuffle rhythms with triplets, you can also notate them using compound time signatures. Compound time signatures have 6, 9, or 12 as the upper number. In popular styles, the lower number is usually an 8. The thing with compound time signatures is that they don't actually have 6, 9, or even 12 beats to the measure. Instead, they're a clever way of writing triplets. To get a handle on compound time signatures, look at 12/8 time, and compare it to 4/4 time. Start with Figure 5-9 (Audio Track 37).

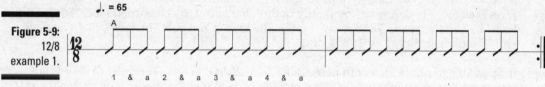

Figure 5-9:
12/8
example 1.

Here are a few things to know about 12/8 time and Figure 5-9:

- In 12/8 time, click tracks are usually set to dotted quarter notes.

- There are three eighth notes per BPM. This is essentially playing eighth-note triplets per BPM.

- 12/8 time does in fact have 12 eighth notes in it, but they're grouped by beams into four groups of three eighth notes each, counted "1 2 3 4 5 6 7 8 9 10 11 12," but "1 and a, 2 and a, 3 and a, 4 a" is also an option and rolls off the tongue better.

- In 12/8 time, musicians tap their feet once per eighth-note group (the first of every three eighth notes), resulting in four taps per measure like that of triplets in 4/4 time. 12/8 count-ins are usually spoken in four as well.

When you go back and listen to Audio Track 30, you hear that it sounds the same as Audio Track 37. As I mention at the beginning of this section, compound time signatures like 12/8 are just a different way to think of and notate triplet-based rhythms.

The long/short feel used in shuffle rhythms like you see in Figure 5-4 and Figure 5-5 can also be written in 12/8 time. In 12/8, you write the rhythm as a quarter note plus an eighth for each beat, as shown in Figure 5-10 (Audio Track 38).

Examples of songs that are triplet-based but typically notated in 12/8 include "Red House" by Jimi Hendrix, "(They Call It) Stormy Monday" by The Allman Brothers Band, "Rumble" by Link Wray, "It's All Right" by The Impressions, "Lovin', Touchin', Squeezin'" by Journey, and "Call Me" by Blondie.

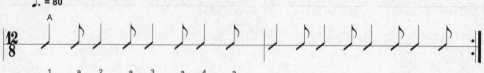

Figure 5-10:
12/8
example 2.

Another compound time signature you may see is 6/8 time. Once again, it's an easy way to write triplet figures, but this time with only two groups of three for each measure. That's like half a measure of triplets in 4/4 time. Sometimes it works better for music publishers to limit the measure length like this, and musicians like to count less when they play. Examples include "You've Got to Hide Your Love Away" by The Beatles, "Breaking the Girl" by Red Hot Chili Peppers, and "Satellite" by Dave Matthews Band.

For the final figure in this chapter, Figure 5-11 (Audio Track 39), you see an example of sixteenth notes in 12/8 time. They're played at exactly twice the rate of 12/8 eighth notes. For this example, it works well to play the eighth notes with all downstrokes and then strike the strings on the way up for the sixteenth notes. The chords and rhythm used here are similar to "The House of the Rising Sun" by The Animals, though the song is played at 82 BPM and the chords are *arpeggiated* (picked through), not strummed. With this many notes at this tempo, it's too much of a mouthful to try to count, so don't bother.

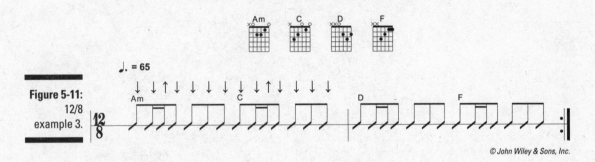

Figure 5-11:
12/8
example 3.

© John Wiley & Sons, Inc.

Because the examples in 12/8 time sound the same as triplets in 4/4 time, you may wonder why it's necessary to use a compound time signature in place of a simple one, or moreover, when it's right to do so. The decision is really up to a composer. There is no real difference in the final sound, but it's often easier to think in eighth notes instead of triplets, and notation is less cluttered when triplet figures are not in constant use.

Odd time signatures and mixed meters

Odd time signatures are ones that have an odd number in the upper position of the fraction. For example, 5/4 and 7/8. Time signatures like this have an irregular feel and can be hard to follow because they don't follow predictable measure lengths. Technically, 3/4 is another example, but it's an exception because waltz time is fairly common. For an example in 5/4, listen to "Living In the Past" by Jethro Tull. You need to count five beats per measure in order to stay on track. Pink Floyd's "Money" is in 7/4 and requires you to count seven beats. Rush's "Subdivisions" starts out in 7/8 time (counting eighth notes now, not quarters).

Something else to look out for is *mixed meter*. This is when a piece of music features more than one time signature, usually with a measure here and there that either adds or drops a beat. For example, the tail end of "Raindrops Keep Fallin' on My Head" by B. J. Thomas adds an extra beat in every other measure for a mixture of 4/4 and 5/4. "All You Need Is Love" by The Beatles drops a beat and alternates between 4/4 and 3/4, as does "Spoonman" by Soundgarden. "Blackbird" by The Beatles features measures of 4/4, 3/4, and even 2/4. The members of the band Rush seem to enjoy both using odd time signatures and mixed meter — these composition techniques are heard in many of their selections, including "Tom Sawyer," "Limelight," and the aforementioned "Subdivisions," to name just a few.

Part III
Fretting-Hand Techniques

Find out how to use a capo in an article at
www.dummies.com/extras/guitarrhythmandtechnique.

Part

Accompanying Techniques

In this part . . .

- ✔ Change up your chord and scale fingerings in order to play to your strengths.

- ✔ Play octaves from rock to jazz.

- ✔ Use hammer-ons, pull-offs, slides, and bends to embellish your riffs and solos.

- ✔ Begin with finger tapping in preparation of dropping jaws.

- ✔ Chime harmonics to sound like angels singing.

- ✔ Use a slide like Bonnie Raitt and play in open tunings like Keith Richards.

Chapter 6

Working with Fingerings

In This Chapter

▶ Changing up your chord fingerings

▶ Exploring scale fingerings

▶ Fretting and playing octaves

▶ Access the audio tracks and video clips at www.dummies.com/go/guitarrhythmtechnique

As the saying goes, there's more than one way to skin a cat. Likewise, you often have options when using your fingers on the guitar fretboard. Maybe you never thought about it, but guitar parts can be performed in any manner that makes them sound good, regardless of whether you use conventional technique. In this chapter, you explore alternate chord and scale fingerings so that you know your options and discover an approach that allows you to play to your strengths.

Change Up: Exploring Optional Chord Fingerings

When you play chord shapes on the guitar, the best fingerings to use are the ones that offer you the most comfort and efficiency. Although there are general rules to follow that benefit everybody, not all guitarists will play everything the same way. Everybody's hands differ slightly in their size, shape, strength, flexibility, and coordination. You should experiment with doing things differently from traditional convention so that you get to know your hands better and discover ways to play to your strengths and work around weaknesses.

 As you work through this section on chords (and the following section on scales), keep in mind that you're not being taught new fingerings that you need to memorize and use. Instead, you're seeing how to think outside the box and finding out how to get the job done in different ways. At the end of the day, whichever fingerings you opt for are up to you. And don't stop with the fingerings covered here! Keep the mindset taught in this chapter with everything that you play.

 When fingering anything on the guitar, don't be concerned about whether your fingering is "correct" or not. Instead, choose whichever options enable you to play and sound your best. If what you play feels right and sounds good, then your fingering is correct!

 If you would like to make your own guitar neck diagrams, get the program Neck Diagrams (www.neckdiagrams.com).

Fingering open chords

To begin, take a look at a few open-position chords and explore some alternate fingerings that you may not have thought of, or perhaps thought were incorrect.

In Figure 6-1, you see four E chord diagrams. The first diagram includes the most common fingering for this chord, the one that is always taught to be "correct." However, you can fret the same notes and produce an identical sound by using the fingering in the second diagram. The only difference is that your second and third fingers have swapped strings. There is nothing wrong with using this fingering if you find it more comfortable to play. The third diagram uses your second finger to hold the second frets of both the fourth and fifth strings. Again, the chord sounds no different than the first two, and if this fingering works better for you, then it's "correct" in your case. The fourth diagram features a variation on the original chord, an E5 power chord that adds an additional fifth, B, in place of the third, G#. Sometimes you want to think outside the box and go for a different chord voicing, too. The same shape can be fretted with your first and fourth fingers, too.

The E5 fingering in Figure 6-1 is probably best played by moving your fretting-hand thumb to the back of the guitar neck (see the nearby sidebar "A rule of thumb").

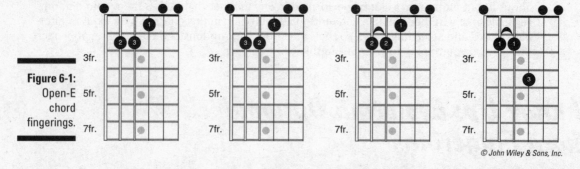

Figure 6-1: Open-E chord fingerings.

© John Wiley & Sons, Inc.

A rule of thumb

Just as important as the placement of your fingers on the fretboard is the placement of your thumb behind it. In fact, sometimes a problem with the fingers is really a problem with the thumb, and some repositioning is in order.

There are three basic positions the thumb can take on the guitar neck:

- **Behind the neck:** Placing your thumb behind the neck is necessary when your fingers need to barre, stretch apart, or reach over to the sixth string. For example, you're not likely to cleanly fret a common E-form barre chord, or play three-notes-per-string major scale patterns without bringing your thumb to the back of the neck. This happens to be the thumb position preferred by classical guitarists, but it's not good for all techniques related to popular styles.

- **Wrapped around the neck:** Wrapping around the neck works well for open-position chords, and playing in small three-finger patterns, like parts of the pentatonic scale. In fact, most pentatonic players will keep their thumbs in the wrapped position until they need to reach for notes on the sixth string with the pinky, in which case they temporarily and quickly move the thumb to the back of the neck. The wrapped position is also necessary if you need to mute or fret strings using the thumb.

- **Somewhere in between:** Most of the time, guitarists use a thumb position that is somewhere in between the preceding two positions, with adjustments always being made as they play to maximize comfort and efficiency.

I show you how to work with the chord fingerings in this section in Video Clip 22.

You don't need to master and use all the fingerings in this chapter. Instead, the goal here is simply to explore your options so that you get to know your own hands better and find what works well for you. You'll progress as a guitarist and refine your skills by playing to your strengths and avoiding your weaknesses.

Next, in Figure 6-2, you try a handful of A-chord options. Basically, your options include some combination of three fingers, or barring with one finger, usually the first. Again, there's no right or wrong way to do things here, as long as you cleanly sound the chord. It's possible that you may favor one fingering in one situation and another fingering in another situation, depending on what chord you come from and where you go. With these fingerings, most guitarists prefer to wrap the fretting-hand thumb around the guitar neck so that it comes up over the top of it on the sixth string side.

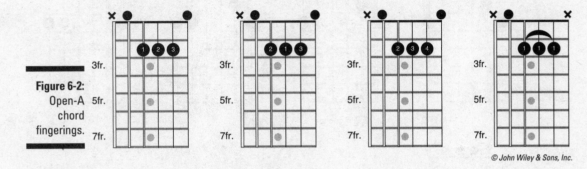

Figure 6-2: Open-A chord fingerings.

© John Wiley & Sons, Inc.

When you play a chord like A in Figure 6-2, wrap your thumb around the back of the guitar neck and graze the sixth string to dampen it so that you clearly hear the open fifth string, A, in the bass position of the chord when strumming.

Next, in Figure 6-3, you see some of your options when playing a D chord in the open position. The first diagram is how a D is usually taught and most often played, but perhaps one of the other versions works better for you. James Taylor favors the example in the second diagram, which you see him use in the "Fire and Rain" guitar lesson on his official YouTube page (`http://youtu.be/OTjd4sna_4o`). The fourth diagram features a fingering that works well if you want to free up your first finger to play an alternate bass note, like F♯ in a D/F♯ chord. Place your first finger on B at the second fret of the fifth string and the same shape makes a Bm7.

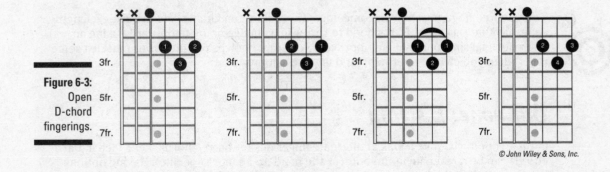

Figure 6-3: Open D-chord fingerings.

© John Wiley & Sons, Inc.

The last chord you look at in the open position is G. Figure 6-4 includes five examples, with the first two being fingerings typically used to initially teach the G chord in beginner guitar lessons. The third diagram is very common and simply swaps the third, B, on the open second string with the fifth, D, at the third fret. If you also remove the B at the second fret of the fifth string, then the chord is all roots and fifths a la a "power chord," a popular voicing favored by rock guitarists. See the fourth diagram and be sure to mute the unwanted fifth string. Finally, the fifth diagram shows you an alternate fingering for the same G5, this time with your thumb coming from behind the neck to fret the root G and your first finger barring both the first and second strings at the third fret. This fingering may seem unusual, but remember to think outside the box. You never know — it may come in handy at some point, or you may need to think creatively in a similar manner with some other chord.

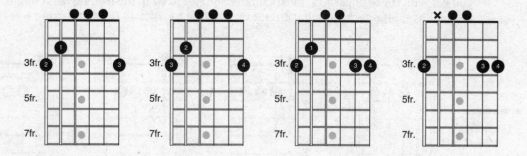

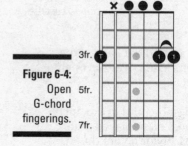

Figure 6-4:
Open G-chord fingerings.

© John Wiley & Sons, Inc.

Although only a few types of open-position chords are covered in this section, you can apply the same ideas to other types of chords that you play near the end of the neck, always thinking outside the box and using fingerings that best help you accomplish what you're trying to play.

Your favored fingerings may become uncomfortable when fatigue sets in during a lengthy song. In situations like this, it's good to throw in a change-up by temporarily using an alternate fingering, one that isn't normally your first choice. You give your muscles some relief when you change your hand and finger positions.

Bar none: E string

In this section, you take a look at alternate fingerings for barre chords. Let's face it, barre chords can be a real pain in the butt (or the hand, to be more specific). Having options helps you to find the fingerings that provide you the most comfort and allow you to avoid stress and strain. In situations where you need to play barre chords for long periods of time, a slight change of position will relieve tension and help you to keep going.

In Figure 6-5, you see a common E-form barre chord played at the fifth fret making an A chord. This, of course, is a movable shape, and you can transpose any of the following examples to chords at other frets. Figure 6-5a, is the standard barre chord shape. Figure 6-5b is the same thing, minus the root on the sixth string. For many guitarists, making this little adjustment makes a huge difference because they don't need to extend the barre across all six strings, and they don't need to keep their fretting-hand thumbs behind the neck. If, like most rockers, you hang your axe low, you'll find that bringing your fretting-hand thumb up around the back of the neck puts your wrist in a far more comfortable position.

Mute all strings that are marked with an "X" in the neck diagrams.

The remainder of the examples in Figure 6-5 show you optional ways in which you can play part or all of this type of barre chord. You probably recognize the example in Figure 6-5d as an F-chord shape, because it's what guitarists often use to play F near the open position at the first fret. Perhaps it never occurred to you that you can use the same shape at other frets for other chords, saving yourself the trouble of playing a whole barre chord.

If you want the root played on the sixth string along with the F shape mentioned earlier, then wrap your thumb around the back of the neck, reach over, and grab it as you see in Figure 6-5e. Jimi Hendrix played most of his barre chords in this manner, with the fifth string thrown in, too, at times, as shown in Figure 6-5f. You find versions of the so-called "Hendrix-style" barre chord in many of Jimi's selections, including "Purple Haze," "The Wind Cries Mary," and "Little Wing." The same technique is used by countless players in rock and other styles.

Figure 6-5g is just a root and fifth power chord. Sometimes there's no need to play any more than it.

In all these diagrams, the numbers represent fingers on your fretting hand, and *T* means thumb. You see me play through all barre chord examples in this section in Video Clip 23. The examples are all based on an A chord at the fifth fret of the sixth string, but you can of course slide the shapes around to play other chords at other frets.

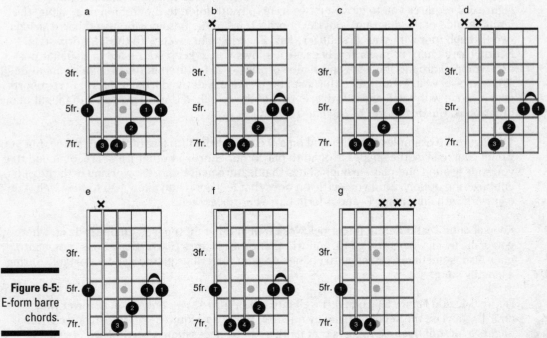

Figure 6-5: E-form barre chords.

In order to put the different fingering options shown in Figure 6-5 to good use, and get a feel for which ones you prefer to play, I recommend that you take some time playing through songs that feature major chords. Any songs will do as long as you can play them by fretting and moving major, E-form barre chords along the sixth string. Think about songs that are played using open-position chords because they can be played using barre chords, too, at least just for practice.

You can play minor versions of the E-form barre chord by lowering the major third on the third string one fret to a minor third. If you're playing a partial form, as shown in Figure 6-5e, then simply remove your second finger and extend your first finger to the third string. Try it!

Bar none: A string

Next you take a look at alternate ways of playing an A-form barre chord, which along with the E form, is one of the most common moveable chord shapes used on guitar. You see the ways it's more commonly played in Figure 6-6.

Figure 6-6a uses your first finger to barre across the fifth fret, really only fretting the needed notes on the first and fifth strings. Your third finger barres partially across the seventh fret, fretting strings two through four. Notice that the sixth string needs to be muted, which can be done by butting up against it with the tip of your first finger as it lays across strings one through five. An optional fingering is to fret strings two through four with individual fingers, specifically fingers two, three, and four, as shown in Figure 6-6b. In either case, you'll probably need your fretting-hand thumb behind the neck.

Depending on your hand, you may have difficulty getting the note on the first string to ring clearly. For this reason, you may choose to leave the first string out by not strumming it as you see in Figure 6-6c. In some cases, it's acceptable to simply play a root and fifth power chord, as shown in Figure 6-6d.

Figure 6-6e removes the fifth string, leaving you with only strings one through four, which can be played with separate fingers, and without needing the thumb behind the neck. Figure 6-6f requires you to move up two frets (pay attention to the fret numbers along the left-hand side of the diagram), put the chord's third in the bass position, and barre strings two through four with your first finger. This fingering pairs well with the "Hendrix-style" E-form barre chord from earlier, because it allows you to keep your hand in a similar position wrapped around the neck and — no surprise — is featured in the previously mentioned Jimi songs as well. Technically, this last chord shape is derived from a G-form barre chord, which, along with the E and A forms, is part of the so-called CAGED system and taught in my other book, *Guitar Theory For Dummies* (Wiley).

The Figure 6-6 examples are all based on a D chord at the fifth fret of the fifth string, but you can of course slide the shapes around to play other chords at other frets. I recommend that you slide around and play through songs that feature major chords, working with the different fingering options until you settle on ones that feel good and allow you to play well. You can work with combining E- and A-form barre chords as well.

Keep in mind that different fingerings work well at different times. It all depends on where you come from, where you go to, and whether other factors (like articulations) come into play. Also, sometimes you need to change up your fingerings just to get comfortable during a lengthy song.

Figure 6-6c and Figure 6-6e convert well into minor forms. You only need to lower the chord's third on the second string by one fret. Doing so requires you to rearrange your fingers a bit, but the nice thing is that neither shape necessitates barring, which usually causes guitarists to strain.

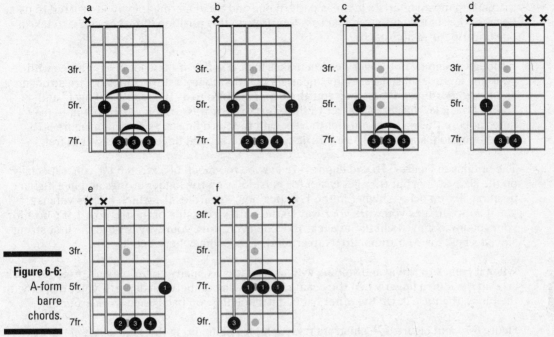

Figure 6-6: A-form barre chords.

This section on chords focuses on just the basics, which include open-position and standard barre chords. There are certainly many other chord types and forms that you play in popular music. When you encounter these chords, remember that there isn't an incorrect way to fret and finger them — ultimately what sounds good is right. Always experiment with optional fingerings in order to find what feels most comfortable to you and allows you to get through a piece of music without straining yourself.

Tipping the Scales: Experimenting with Different Scale Fingerings

In this section, you explore a few ways to finger common scale patterns, take a look at how fingerings change from position to position, and work toward finding finger combinations that work well for you and allow you to play at your best. More than just getting through the examples that follow, you take away ideas that help you navigate your way through other scales and scale applications you come up against as a guitar player.

Pent-up frustration: Fingering pentatonic scales

Pentatonic patterns are extremely common in popular music, especially the rock and blues genres. They're used to play melodies, riffs, lead guitar solos, and bass lines. You get started with this scale in *Guitar Theory For Dummies*. In this book, you work with the techniques that often accompany the scale, with this section in particular focusing on how you finger the patterns.

In Figure 6-7, you see some optional fingerings for a few of the pentatonic scale patterns (namely, patterns one, two, and four, as taught in *Guitar Theory For Dummies*). Figure 6-7a is the pattern most guitarists learn as pattern one and the fingering they're instructed to use. Because the scale tones stretch across four frets in this position, it makes sense to take a one-finger-per-fret approach.

Although assigning one finger per fret makes logical sense, it may not always agree with your fine motor skill senses. Many guitarists find that their first three fingers are stronger and more coordinated than their fourth finger (referred to as the "rubbish finger" and "God's little joke" by shred master Guthrie Govan). For this reason, it's common to play notes at both the seventh and eighth frets with the third finger, as shown in Figure 6-7b. Another option, shown in Figure 6-7c, is to use your second finger at the seventh fret.

The options in Figure 6-7b and Figure 6-7c may be too much of a stretch for you, especially on the sixth string, but they get easier for most folks on the higher strings and in a higher position, like an octave higher in the 17th position. Regardless of which fingers you use, you'll notice that as you work your way to the sixth string side of the fretboard, it's best for your thumb to move behind the neck, and when you work your way toward the first string side, it's best for your thumb to wrap around or rest somewhere in between.

When it comes to riffing and soloing with scale patterns, many guitar players prefer to work around the fourth finger when they can; some actually do better using it. If you prosper with the pinky, then use it. On the other hand, if it's holding you back, then work around it.

Figure 6-7d and Figure 6-7e illustrate two examples of fingering the same scale in the next position in the shape of what's commonly called pattern two. You see that you can take either a one-finger-per-fret approach, or remove your fourth finger from the equation and play it all with your first three fingers. Another option, which is not shown, is to play the whole pattern using only your first and third fingers. Typically, when this pattern is in use, players focus on the notes in the higher register, strings one through three, and use their first three fingers in some combination, with the thumb wrapped. This works well when hammering on, pulling off, and bending, articulations that require more dexterity than many people's fourth finger can handle.

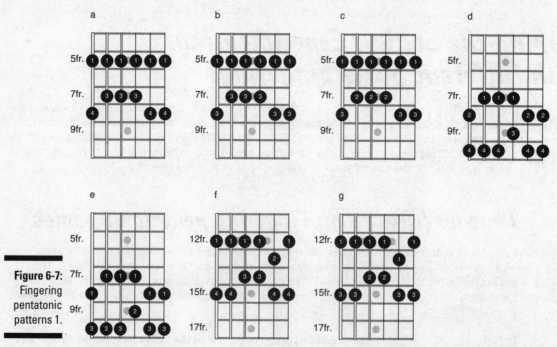

Figure 6-7: Fingering pentatonic patterns 1.

Proper fingerings

You'll often hear different opinions about how guitarists should or should not finger certain passages. Some may even allege that there is always a proper guitar fingering for each musical situation. Maybe you find yourself falling into this way of thinking. For example, you may think that it's more "correct" to use the pinky whenever possible, or at least it's a bad habit to avoid using it. But many famous guitarists, including Stevie Ray Vaughan, Eddie Van Halen, and Eric Johnson, play a great deal of their lead guitar solos with their first three fingers. On the other hand, players such as Paul Gilbert, Steve Morse, and John Petrucci seem to favor patterns that require a lot of pinky action. Obviously, the idea that there is a universally correct and proper fingering for guitarists to use with everything is not true.

You should always work with a fingering that produces the best results for you, even if it means using something unconventional. As long as the end result sounds good, then the fingering is correct! If you fumble and falter and things don't come out right, then you need to reexamine your fingering and determine whether you need to choose another one or work on getting your fingers in better shape. While you have options, don't use your options as a copout to developing good technique. If your inclination is to use only your first finger for everything you play, obviously you won't get very far and working with more fingers is in order. There are even times when using the fourth finger can lead to the best results if you're patient and put the time into practicing with it.

Figure 6-7f and Figure 6-7g jump two positions ahead to what most players call pattern four. This puts you in the 12th position. Because the frets are closer together, using all four fingers can get too crowded. From this position on the neck and onward, it works well to use fewer fingers with the pinky being the first to go. You can try the fingering illustrated in Figure 6-7g or any other combination that feels good to you.

As you know, the pentatonic scale creates five different patterns on the guitar fretboard and is played in all keys. I only use three of these patterns in my examples, and the sample key of A minor/C major, but the same concept applies to all patterns and in all keys.

You see me demonstrate all the scale fingering options from this section in Video Clip 24.

Next, in Figure 6-8, you play through a sample pentatonic riff using different patterns in different positions. And "riff" is a bit of an exaggeration because there isn't much to this part. The real point of this exercise is to demonstrate that there's often more than one way to arrange parts on the fretboard, and you should always use positions and fingerings that work well for you. Keep this in mind with everything that you play. You need to follow the tab with this figure in order to play each version of the riff in the intended position. The fingering is up to you. By now a natural fingering ought to fall into place. You can repeat the fingerings I use in Video Clip 24 or try your own.

In Figure 6-9, you play an exercise similar to the last one but in the next register of the scale. I tabbed out five examples in five different positions, though there are more ways to play the part. For example, the second example that begins in measure three can use the open G string in place of the G note at the fifth fret of the fourth string. Other examples can shift back into another pattern instead of staying all in one position. You have fingering options, too. (Remember how you tried one finger per fret, three fingers, and two fingers in the previous section.)

You may be wondering how you'll know what parts look like position to position as you work through passages on your own. You have a few options:

- ✔ Use your ear and trial and error to find pitches as you transpose from one position to the next.

- ✔ Examine what the actual note names of a given part are, and then locate the same notes in the next position.

- ✔ Identify what type of scale pattern a part is based in and move to the next pattern in the same scale.

Figure 6-8:
Fingering
pentatonic
patterns 2.

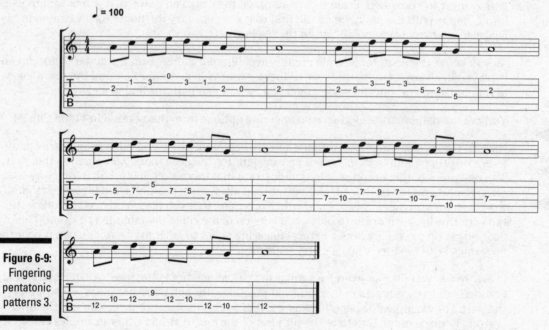

Figure 6-9:
Fingering
pentatonic
patterns 3.

Most guitarists use a combination of the three options to get around, which is why it's good to know a bit about pitches, notes, and patterns.

Explore your options when not only playing the figures in this chapter, but with everything you play. A guitar part that is awkward for you to play may feel much better when you rethink the fingering and rearrange the position.

Major leagues: Fingering major scales

This section is similar to the last except it focuses on major scale patterns, which include more notes and half-steps (and are covered in *Guitar Theory For Dummies*). You take a look at the different ways to finger patterns and play in positions. The purpose here is to know the process that helps you choose fingerings and arrange parts, so you find what feels right and play to your strengths.

In Figure 6-10, you see two versions of five G-major scale patterns, with the numbers indicating fingerings. There are, of course, more ways to play major scales than this, but these examples are enough to get the point across about fingering options. The first diagram in each set features commonly taught fingerings that utilize the fourth finger, ones that follow a traditional one-finger-per-fret approach where possible and require your thumb to be placed behind the neck. The second diagram in each set features an optional fingering, one that eliminates the fourth finger and may afford you the opportunity to wrap your thumb. You see me play through all examples from this section in Video Clip 25. Notice how my thumb position changes, and that I sometimes use my first finger twice in a row by sliding it up or down by a half-step.

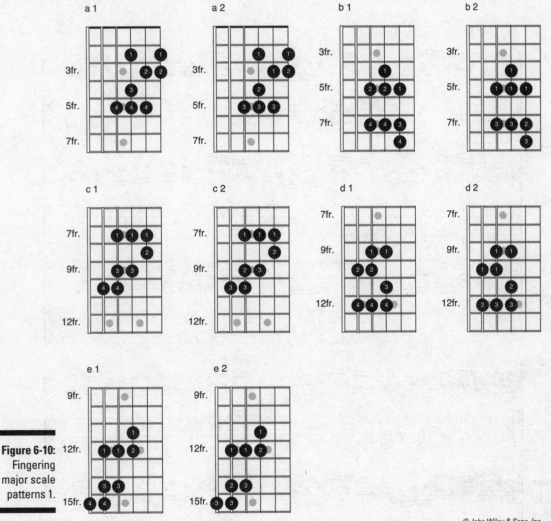

Figure 6-10: Fingering major scale patterns 1.

Personally, I favor the second examples in each set when I riff and jam, and I often see other players do so as well, but you may feel more comfortable with the more traditional fingerings, or perhaps some other combination not illustrated. Again, these examples are really an exercise in exploring your options — play through them for a while until you settle on fingerings that work well for you.

Try playing through the Figure 6-10 examples as fast as you can. You may find that your preferred fingerings don't work as well when you need to pick up the pace, and a change is in order. Keep this in mind when you work on fast passages.

The examples in this section feature select patterns in the key of G, but you can apply the same concept in other major scale patterns and keys, always exploring your options and choosing what works well for you.

Next, in Figure 6-11, you work with a melodic idea by repeating it in each of the five pattern positions from the previous figure. As you go, use the fingering examples in Figure 6-10, trying both the ones with and without the fourth finger, to see what gives you the best results. You can also put together new fingerings of your own if something else works better for you. This figure is set to just 65 BPM, but you can try faster tempos too, which may affect your fingering choices.

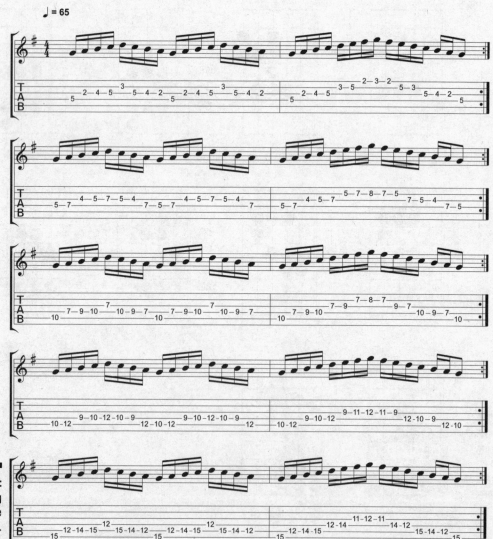

Figure 6-11: Fingering major scale patterns 2.

Although the exercises are written all as one piece of music, you should stick with just one line of the music at a time, repeating it until you settle on a fingering and play it fluently. You may find that you play some lines better than others, an indication that the particular positions and patterns are a good fit for you. As you play major scale parts, including the minor scale and modes that are based in the same patterns (see *Guitar Theory For Dummies*), work the areas on the fretboard in which you feel most comfortable.

Playing Octaves

While you're on the topic of fingering scales, it's a good time to take a look at playing octaves, a very popular guitar technique that has some challenges to address.

Octaves are higher and lower occurrences of the same note. For example, G at the third fret of the sixth string and G at the fifth fret of the fourth string are an octave apart. It's common for guitar players to hold octaves like this, and then move their hands up and down the fretboard to play melodies, riffs, and solos with different notes.

Holding and sounding octaves is fairly simple to do if you fingerpick and pluck the two strings with a thumb and finger, but believe it or not, this is not how octaves are usually played. Instead, most guitarists strum octaves using a flatpick and mute the unwanted strings (that is, the strings other than the ones on which you're fretting notes) by leaning their fingers back and using a damping technique. In this case, the scratching sound that the strumming and damping causes is used to good effect. Combined with the fretted notes, the scratching makes a thicker sound.

The best way to illustrate the damping technique is to use X's in guitar tab, though you won't always see them used in transcribed scores because it's assumed you know to mute and damp strings when playing octaves. In Figure 6-12, you see octave shapes that climb up the first four degrees of the G-major scale, with quarters on each pair of notes for a full measure. To begin, just look at the first beat of measure one. Follow my example in Video Clip 26 and take note of the following special points:

Figure 6-12:
Playing
octaves 1.

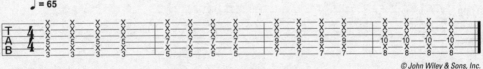

© John Wiley & Sons, Inc.

- ✔ The numbers indicate where to fret and play actual notes — in this case, G's an octave apart. Most players will use their first finger on the G at the third fret of the sixth string and then either their third or fourth finger on the G at the fifth fret of the fourth string. Personally, I like to use my fourth finger for octaves as you see me do in Video Clip 26.

- ✔ The X's represent strings that are strummed, but damped. You dampen the strings by leaning your fingers back so that the underside of the fingers lightly touch the unused strings, cutting them off so that they don't ring. As you lean your fingers back, be sure to keep your fingertips on the notes that ought to be fretted and played. When your hand is in the right position, you can strum across all the strings only hearing the desired pitches. The rest of the strings will produce only the sound of scratching. This technique takes a while to develop. At first, you're likely to hear unwanted string noise, or have trouble sounding the notes that should be heard. You may initially struggle with applying pressure on some strings while simultaneously relaxing on others, but the more you work with this technique, the cleaner it will sound.

✔ When you get a handle on playing G octaves in the first measure of Figure 6-12, you move on to the other measures and up the fretboard and scale. I use part of the G scale for this example, but you can play octaves with the same fingering anywhere on the sixth string.

TIP

As you play the octaves in Figure 6-12, you really only need to strum across strings six, five, and four. But if you should strum more strings than that, make sure they're properly damped.

The example in Figure 6-13 is the same as the last, only moved over a string ascending a partial C scale. You use the same techniques to fret and dampen the strings, but in this case you need to add one or two more details. Since the sixth string is now damped, you need to get something on it. Most players will fret the notes on the fifth string with the back half of their fingertip so that the front half butts up against the sixth string, keeping it quiet. Another option is to reach over to the sixth string with your unused second finger. You see me damp both ways in Video Clip 26. Jimi Hendrix strummed the same kind of octave shapes on the fifth string as well as the previous ones on the sixth string in his songs "Fire" and "Third Stone from the Sun."

Figure 6-13:
Playing
octaves 2.

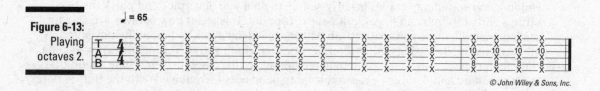

© John Wiley & Sons, Inc.

Figure 6-14 is one final example of playing octave shapes, this time with your first finger placed on the fourth and third strings. Because these octave shapes reach to and over the second string, and because of the way the second string is tuned one fret lower than the other strings, you need to reach up an additional fret in order to reach the octaves. You also need to reach over with your unused second finger to help mute idle strings.

Figure 6-14:
Playing
octaves 3.

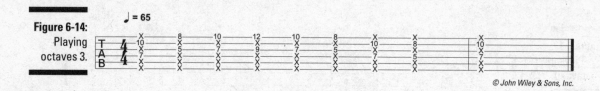

© John Wiley & Sons, Inc.

Figure 6-14 is set to eighth notes and moves through the A-minor pentatonic scale. You may find it helpful to play only the first-finger notes in the lower register first, just to map out the basic movement of the passage, then add in the fourth finger to complete the octaves. This figure is also demonstrated in Video Clip 26. Jazz guitar legend Wes Montgomery used A-minor pentatonic octaves in his song "Bumpin' on Sunset." He was famous for strumming across the strings with the pad of his right thumb for a mellow, jazzy sound.

Now that you know how to rethink your fingerings, go attack some chord changes, riffs, and solos!

Chapter 7

Adding Articulation and Expression

- -

In This Chapter

▶ Playing hammer-ons, pull-offs, slides, and bends

▶ Developing vibrato

▶ Tapping with two hands

▶ Using grace notes

▶ Access the audio tracks and video clips at www.dummies.com/go/guitarrhythmtechnique

- -

*I*n music, *articulation* refers to the performance techniques used to sound and transition between notes. On guitar, this includes hammering fingers onto and pulling fingers off of the strings, sliding between notes, and bending strings to change pitches. In this chapter, you work with these various ways of playing and connecting notes, along with using expressive techniques like vibrato and grace notes. Additionally, you see how all these techniques are notated in guitar tab and used in popular songs.

Working with Articulations

As you begin working with articulations, you find out that playing notes on the guitar fretboard can involve a lot more than simply pressing down a string and plucking it. The fingers on your fretting hand in particular can contribute in a variety of ways, even doing the work of your picking hand by sounding notes. Remember the sore fingers you experienced as a newcomer to guitar, before your calluses developed? Well, you're likely to have tender fingers again as you work with the techniques in this chapter that stress your fingers in new ways. As the saying goes, no pain no gain. You'll increase your finger strength and improve your dexterity, as well as give your guitar playing more expression.

Hammering it out: Using hammer-ons

An alternative to plucking a string to sound a note on guitar is to quickly tap a finger onto a string and down to the fretboard. In most cases, this is done while a string is in vibration. For example, pluck an open string with your pick in a normal manner, and then, while the string is still ringing, use a fret-hand finger to sharply press down on the same string at a higher fret so that a new pitch is sounded. This technique is called a *hammer-on* or *hammering on*. When you do it right, the force of your finger will put the string into motion again, thus maintaining the vibration and sustain.

In Figure 7-1, you see how you can ascend an E-minor/G-major pentatonic scale in the open position (pattern one, as I teach it in *Guitar Theory For Dummies*) by plucking the open strings and hammering on the fretted notes at the third and second frets. In guitar tablature, hammer-ons are tied. With these ties, you play the first fret number and then sound the next without plucking the string again but instead hammering onto it.

Figure 7-1:
Playing hammer-ons.

© John Wiley & Sons, Inc.

Before you play through the whole figure as written, work with each hammer-on one at a time, repeating each one until you execute the technique properly. You can use your first, second, or third finger to hammer into the fretted notes. I suggest you start with your first finger and stick with it until the hammering on is smooth; then train your other fingers to do it, too. You can follow my demonstration in Video Clip 27, footage that includes all hammer-on, pull-off, trill, and slide examples in this chapter. In the second half of Figure 7-1, you play the same hammer-ons but starting at the other end on the first string and working your way back to the sixth string.

One thing to be careful of when playing hammer-ons is creating unwanted noise. Be sure to use parts of both hands to keep idle strings quiet so that you hear only the intended pitches.

Playing Pink Floyd's "Wish You Were Here" is an easy way to get started with hammer-ons in the open position. The song opens with a 12-string acoustic guitar using some forms of Em and G along with a pentatonic scale and hammer-ons. You can play the part on a standard six-string acoustic or electric guitar. You see something similar in Figure 7-2. Follow along with my demonstration in Video Clip 27. Tesla's "What You Give" is another example.

Figure 7-2:
Playing a hammer-on riff.

© John Wiley & Sons, Inc.

Lynyrd Skynyrd's "Sweet Home Alabama" also opens with a guitar using hammer-ons in the open position. The same song later features a repeating and circular hammer-on lick during the chorus, one that is reminiscent of the guitar solo in "A Hard Day's Night" by The Beatles.

Hammer-ons aren't just for playing riffs. Rhythm guitar players use them to embellish the chords they play. Next, in Figure 7-3, you play in a country style by hammering into the third of each major chord in the key of C in the open position.

Figure 7-3: Hammering on with open-position chords.

You can take the idea from Figure 7-3 and hammer into any fingered note in any open-position chord that you play. For example, Willie Nelson hammers into the note B at the second fret of the fifth string while holding an E-major chord in his song "On the Road Again." You hammer on to A at the second fret of the third string when playing Sublime's "What I Got." You hear portions of Am and D chords hammered into in Tom Petty's "Mary Jane's Last Dance."

In Figure 7-4, you return to the E-minor/G-major pentatonic scale pattern from earlier, but this time an octave higher in the 12th position, and only using the fifth, fourth, and third strings. In this example, you need to fret the first note on each string with your first finger, and then hammer into the second notes with your third finger. Once you get used to this technique, try playing the opening riff to "Paranoid" by Black Sabbath.

Figure 7-4: Hammering in the 12th position.

It's important that you not lift your first finger when hammering on, or you'll cut off the string and make it harder to sound the hammered note.

Pentatonic scale patterns, which are taught in *Guitar Theory For Dummies,* work well for practicing hammer-ons because they typically feature two notes per string. You can play the first note on each string in a normal manner, and then hammer into the second note. Just be sure to hold onto the first note as you hammer onto the next so that you don't cut off the string. Not only will hammering your way through all five pentatonic patterns help you to learn the scale and fretboard positions, but it's a great workout to improve finger strength and dexterity. Try it!

Pulling your weight: Using pull-offs

The opposite of the hammer-on is the *pull-off*. This is where you pull your finger off a note in a manner that also plucks the string, putting the string back into motion so as to sound the next note, whether it be an open string or a note fretted by some other finger. In Figure 7-5, you descend the E-minor pentatonic scale by picking only the fretted notes and then pulling off to the open strings.

Figure 7-5:
Playing
pull-offs.

© John Wiley & Sons, Inc.

To begin Figure 7-5, you fret and pick the G at the third fret of the first string in a normal manner, and then sound the E note on the open first string in a new way, by plucking the string with your fret-hand finger as you *pull* it away from the third fret.

When playing a pull-off, it's important to point out that you can't simply lift your fret-hand finger — this will cut off the string and fail to sound the next note. Instead, you have to use your fret-hand finger to pluck the string and sound the next note. You may kick your finger forward or snap it backward as you lift it away, whichever method feels most comfortable to you and cleanly sounds the next note. Be sure to avoid bumping into neighboring strings and causing unwanted noise, and be sure to use parts of both hands to mute the strings that aren't in use.

Like hammer-ons, pull-offs are also marked in tab with a tie. You know the difference between the two by which direction you move on the fretboard. If the numbers in the tab increase, you hammer-on, or rather hammer *up* to the higher fret. If the numbers decrease, you pull-off or pull *down* to the lower fret.

You can practice each string in Figure 7-5 individually and at your own pace first; then work on connecting them to complete the scale. When you're ready, follow along with me in Video Clip 27.

In the second half of Figure 7-5, you take the same example up an octave and play in the 12th position. In this case, you must fret all the notes to which you pull off, and a finger needs to be in place *before* you execute the technique. For example, get your first finger in position at the 12th fret of the first string; *then* use another finger, probably your third or fourth finger, to fret and pull off from the 15th fret. If your first finger is not in place before you pull off, you'll fumble through the figure and fail to cleanly sound each note. This remains true for all the pull-offs in Figure 7-5, and all pull-offs you play on guitar in general. Pull-offs are used with the pentatonic scale like this in all blues and rock music styles.

The pentatonic scale works well for practicing pull-offs. You can descend all five patterns using pull-offs.

Open-position chords can be embellished with pull-offs, too. You see an example in Figure 7-6 that features the chords D and A. Each measure begins with a sus4 chord, with the fourth pulled off to each chord's normal third. Each measure ends with the thirds pulled off making sus2 chords. You may need to rearrange your fingers on the A chord halfway through the measure in order to get in the best position to perform the pull-offs. Watch how I do it in Video Clip 27. Similar techniques are heard in Led Zeppelin's "Stairway to Heaven" and James Taylor's "Fire and Rain."

Next, in Figure 7-7, you use pull-offs to play triads, outlining the chords Bm and F♯. The famous guitar solo section to "Hotel California" by the Eagles ends with dual guitars using the same technique. Mark Knopfler does something similar in his "Sultans of Swing" solo at a much faster rate and using triads related to the D-minor scale. With pull-offs, it's often easier to play faster because more notes can roll off of your fingertips without your needing to pick them all.

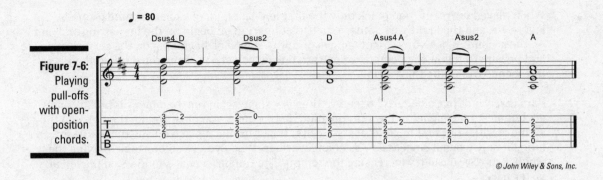

Figure 7-6:
Playing
pull-offs
with open-
position
chords.

© John Wiley & Sons, Inc.

Figure 7-7:
Pulling off
California-
style.

© John Wiley & Sons, Inc.

Now that you know how to play both hammer-ons and pull-offs, you can combine them to play a common guitar lick where you fret and pluck a note normally, follow it up with a hammer-on, and then finish it off with a pull-off. Altogether, you sound notes three times with just one stroke of the pick — an efficient trick. You know to sound notes with hammer-ons and pull-offs like this when they're all tied together, an indication that the notes are to be sounded without replucking the string.

In Figure 7-8, you add one more note to this lick, a fretted and plucked one on the neighboring string, making a four-note group that you should repeat slowly at your own pace until you can combine all the notes and techniques into one continuous movement. The famous lead guitar riff featured in "Layla" by Derek and The Dominos is built off of a very similar lick in the key of D minor.

Figure 7-8:
Combining
hammer-ons
and pull-offs.

© John Wiley & Sons, Inc.

When played correctly, you pluck only the first and last note of each four-note group in Figure 7-8, and the first three notes are a triplet figure. You begin on the first string and end on the second. When you're ready, move onto the same lick beginning on the second string, and be sure to follow the pentatonic pattern one, which starts at the third fret and ends at the second fret of the third string.

Bars three and four of Figure 7-8 feature the very same scale run, hammer-on/pull-offs and all, but an octave higher in the 12th position. In this case, you must fret all the notes at the 12th fret with your first finger. Keep your first finger firmly in place during the whole lick, lifting it only when it's necessary to change strings. When you're comfortable playing the whole figure, you can try increasing the tempo. The run has a neat sound when played at a faster pace.

The pentatonic scale works well for combining hammer-ons and pull-offs. You can ascend and descend any one of the five patterns in any key by plucking the first note on each string, hammering onto the next, and then pulling right back off. Try it!

Next, in Figure 7-9, you play in the style of "Tears in Heaven" by Eric Clapton, embellishing a few standard open-position chords with hammer-ons and pull-offs. You hear similar techniques and the chords D, A, and Bm used in Rush's "The Trees" around the 0:35 mark.

Figure 7-9:
Combining hammer-ons and pull-offs with chords.

© John Wiley & Sons, Inc.

In some cases, guitarists will play a rapid series of alternating hammer-ons and pull-offs between a pair of notes called a *trill*. The individual notes in a trill don't have a specific note value, their value is as fast as you can play them, though you do repeat the trill for a specified length of time.

You see trill examples in Figure 7-10 based in E-minor pentatonic. I begin with hammer-ons and pull-offs set to steady sixteenth notes in the first measure, and then switch to a free-time trill in the second measure, so that you see and hear the difference between playing in and out of time. In the second measure, increase your hammer-on/pull-off rate to as fast as you can, being sure to still execute the techniques cleanly.

Figure 7-10:
Playing a trill 1.

© John Wiley & Sons, Inc.

Notice that trills are notated with only the primary note — in this case, the open fourth string, and the alternate note, second fret, in parentheses. Above this is *tr* and a squiggly vibrato line. Using this method saves the score from getting cluttered up with excessive notes, and saves you the trouble of trying to read, count, and play them all. Repeat a trill for the duration of the note value that it's written in — in this case, a whole note.

Measures three and four of Figure 7-10 repeat the same exercise an octave higher in the 12th position where both notes in the trill need to be fretted. Again you start with steady sixteenth notes, and then switch to a sort of free time for the trill. As always, make sure to sound only the intended notes and position your hands in a manner to silence unwanted noise from other strings. Stevie Ray Vaughan used this same type of trill all the time while playing in his favored pentatonic boxes. Listen to the beginning of "Say What?" or the 0:38 mark of "Little Wing" or the 4:26 mark of "Couldn't Stand the Weather" for a few examples.

You can trill between any two notes in any pentatonic pattern in any key. Try it!

Slip slidin' away: Using slides

Sliding is a technique where you keep your fingers pressed down to the fretboard as you move to a new fret, sustaining the strings as you go. In tab, two fret numbers that are connected with a slide have a line in between them that either goes in an upward or downward direction depending on the change in pitch. When you are not to pluck the pitch that the slide ends on, then the two fret numbers are also connected with a tie, much like a hammer-on or pull-off, as you see in Figure 7-11, an example played somewhat in the style of "Iron Man" by Black Sabbath.

Figure 7-11: Sliding power chords.

© John Wiley & Sons, Inc.

Notice that the two groups of notes connected by a slide in Figure 7-11 are set to eighth notes. You fret and pluck the first group, a D5, on beat three, then slide up a whole-step to an E5 on the "and" of beat three. The slide itself is the only means of producing the notes. See how I do it in Video Clip 27.

To properly execute the slide technique, you must apply enough pressure to sustain the notes, but relax enough to slide across the strings. You develop the right touch to slide the more you do it.

You see another example of sliding in Figure 7-12. This time, you fret and pluck a note in a normal manner, and then follow it with two slides: one down a whole-step and another right back up to your starting position. Make sure that you sound the first note loudly enough so as to have enough string vibration to carry you through the slides that follow. This example is also set to eighth notes, so be sure to slide to each destination at the right time in order to sound each note on its particular part of the beat. Each group of three notes that is connected by slides is followed by a plucked note on a neighboring string. You can start the slide group with any finger you like and move to the last note in each measure with any finger you like, though it may work better to start with one finger and end with another. Your call.

Figure 7-12: Sliding in the pentatonic scale.

© John Wiley & Sons, Inc.

Figure 7-12 makes its way through an A-minor pentatonic scale much in the same way Tom Petty's "Breakdown" does. Follow along with me in Video Clip 27.

When lead lines are played in a very flowing manner with notes connected using a lot of hammer-ons, pull-offs, and slides, it's called *legato*.

Fall from grace: Using grace notes

In music, not all notes have values. In some situations you use a pitch to quickly lead into another, and it's sounded only for a very brief moment. This is called a *grace note*. Grace notes are written in a score as smaller notes set slightly apart from the primary ones. They aren't counted and don't contribute to a measure's number of beats.

Notes quickly played around central notes are called *ornaments* or *embellishments*. They serve to decorate or "ornament" a note. A grace note is a type of ornament.

On guitar, grace notes are often the first pitch of an immediate hammer-on as shown in Figure 7-13. The idea in this example is to play an E5 but lead into it with another pitch. As you put your first and third fingers into place to play the common power chord shape, barre with your first finger to cover both the sixth and fifth strings. Then, instead of sounding the chord tones straight up, strum the strings without your third (fret hand) finger, which means that you hear the A note under your first finger at the 12th fret of the fifth string, then immediately hammer into the 14th fret of the fifth string. Although the tab seems to indicate that the 12th fret of the fifth string is played first and by itself, both strings and the hammer-on happen together on each downbeat. You hear the sound of grace notes in Video Clip 27. A similar technique is used in Black Sabbath's "Paranoid."

Figure 7-13: Grace note hammer-on 1.

© John Wiley & Sons, Inc.

Figure 7-14 is another grace note example, one that features quick hammer-ons used to embellish an F major played as a partial barre chord in the first position. Again, the grace notes — the notes from which you hammer — have no note values. Instead, they occur directly on the beats along with the other notes and the hammer-ons immediately follow them. With a little finger rearranging, you can move these licks around the fretboard as Jimi Hendrix does in "The Wind Cries Mary." Follow my demonstration in Video Clip 27.

Figure 7-14: Grace note hammer-on 2.

© John Wiley & Sons, Inc.

Figure 7-15 features some E-minor pentatonic riffing much in the style of Jimi Hendrix's "Purple Haze" and Led Zeppelin's "Whole Lotta Love." The primary pitch that begins each measure is preceded by a grace note slide from a whole-step lower. Remember that the grace notes have no note values and are slid directly into the next note on the same part of the beat. When you fret the grace notes with your third finger and slide up a whole-step, then you perfectly position yourself to complete each phrase. That's what I do in Video Clip 27.

Figure 7-15: Grace note slide.

© John Wiley & Sons, Inc.

Bending the rules: Using bends

Bending is the technique of pushing or pulling a string out of alignment, thus increasing the tension and raising the pitch. Bends are distinctive to guitar and have an expressive quality that is vocal-like. Most blues, country, and rock-based guitar solos feature bends within a pentatonic scale as you see in Figure 7-16. I demonstrate this bend as well as this section's other bends in Video Clip 28.

An upward-arching arrow is used to notate a bent note in tablature with either *full* or *1* above it to indicate how far the pitch should rise in musical steps. Because this example requires you to raise the pitch a whole step, it's a good idea to take a moment to play the destination pitch first so that you know what you're reaching for, or rather what you're bending to. Your goal is to make the seventh fret of the third string sound like the ninth fret. In order to put this bend into context, I've added an A-minor pentatonic run in the second measure. You then return to the same bend in measure three. The same bend starts out the guitar solo in Led Zeppelin's "Stairway to Heaven."

Figure 7-16: Whole-step bend.

The key in this example is A minor and the bend is from a fourth interval to a fifth interval. Normally in this situation, you fret the note on the third string with your third finger, but place your second finger on the string as well to help push the string toward the sixth string side of the fretboard. As you push, you take the neighboring strings along with you, being sure not to let them slip over your fingertips, which will cause unwanted noise and scrape against your cuticles. Your first finger can relax and lay across the strings on the nut side of the bend, putting a damper on any strings not in use.

Most players prefer to wrap their thumbs around the back of the neck, bringing it up over the top of the fretboard edge, and squeeze their hand together as if they were wringing out a sponge or exercising their forearm with a fitness hand grip. That said, there's no right or wrong way to bend a string — whatever sounds good is right, and you see some variation between pro players.

String gauge and bending

In order to bend strings on a guitar, you need to use a light gauge of strings. *String gauge* refers to the thickness of the guitar string — the larger the gauge, the heavier the string. Thickness is measured in thousandths of an inch, and string sets are categorized by the gauge of the first string specifically. Typically, electric guitars are strung with a set of strings that include a first string measuring 0.009, or a set of "9s" as guitarists usually say. Strings this size or lighter are fairly easy to bend. String gauges heavier than this are harder to bend and require a well-conditioned hand with extra-thick calluses. Because acoustic guitars are designed to produce a maximum amount of acoustic volume, as opposed to an electric, which benefits from magnetic pickups and amplification, they're strung with heavier-gauge strings. These strings may produce a better acoustic tone, but they're very hard, sometimes impossible, to bend. As you work through this section on bends, use a guitar strung with light-gauge strings, like an electric, or restring an acoustic with extra-light strings, being sure to not use a wound third string.

Something else to take into consideration as you work with bends is the strength of your fingers and the thickness of your calluses. Bending puts tremendous pressure on your fingertips, taxing your hand well beyond what ordinary playing does. Your fingers will get sore as you practice bending. As you strengthen your muscles and thicken your calluses, bending will become easier and feel more comfortable.

One final point to make, it's fairly common in rock music for guitarists to tune all of their strings down by a half-step. This lowers the sixth string, E, to E♭ (hence, the name *E♭ tuning*). This tuning's popularity is based on a few things:

- Some players find the slightly lower tonality to be preferential.

- Singers are better able to hit the high notes.

- Lowering the tuning loosens the strings and makes bending easier!

E♭ tuning is used on Jimi Hendrix's "Voodoo Child (Slight Return)," Guns N' Roses' "Sweet Child O' Mine," and Stevie Ray Vaughan's "Pride and Joy" just to name a few.

Figure 7-17 is an example where you only bend up a half-step, in this case from B at the seventh fret of the first string to C at the eighth fret. Notice the little half fraction (½) above the bend. This phrase is centered on a G chord in D form. I demonstrate for you in Video Clip 28. You hear a similar half-step bend used in "Sweet Child o' Mine" by Guns N' Roses around the 2:56 mark (guitars tuned down one half-step to E♭).

Figure 7-17: Half-step bend.

Other types of bends to look out for are ¼ bends, where you only bend halfway to the next semitone, also called a *microtone,* and bends beyond a whole tone like 1½ and 2. The guitar solos in Pink Floyd's "Another Brick in the Wall (Part II)" and Jimi Hendrix's "All Along the Watchtower" both feature bends that stretch beyond a whole step. Just beware, the higher the bend, the harder the bend. Better play it safe until you're ready to stretch the limits of your strings and hand.

Next you look at a *bend and release,* a type of bend in which you hear the bend return to its starting position without being cut off. You'll know when to allow a bend to release when you see not only an arrow going up in tab, but also one going back down. You see an example in Figure 7-18. You bend up a whole step at the 14th fret of the third string on beat one, release the bend on the "and" of beat one so that you hear the pitch, A, at the 14th fret no bend, and then finish the phrase with a few notes played in a normal manner. Keep in mind that in order to hear the bend return to its starting point, you must continue to sustain the string through the bend and release. Watch me do it in Video Clip 28. Eric Clapton used a similar bend and release in his famous opening to "Wonderful Tonight."

One more type of bend to familiarize yourself with is the *prebend.* With this technique, you start with the string in the bent position before you strike it. In my Figure 7-19 example (Video Clip 28), the prebend is connected to a bend and release. So, you prebend and then hear it release. Another way to think of it is as a *reverse bend.* You hear the string come down, not up.

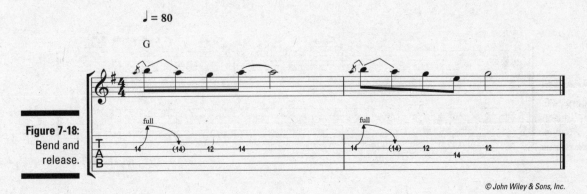

Figure 7-18: Bend and release.

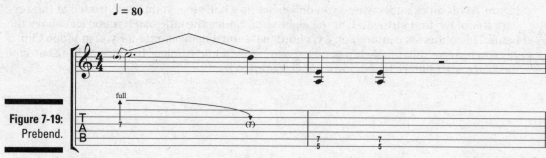

Figure 7-19:
Prebend.

© John Wiley & Sons, Inc.

In tablature, a prebend is notated with an arrow that stands perfectly vertical, indicating that the bend is already up at the moment you strike the string. In my example, this is followed by a downward-pointing arrow, representing the release of the bend and a return of the string and pitch to its normal fretted position. Perhaps the most recognizable example of a prebend and release is "Wild Thing" by The Animals, which starts off in a manner very similar to Figure 7-19. Ace Frehley introduces the first lead-guitar licks of Kiss's "Deuce" with a prebend and release at 1:00 that is then followed by a pull-off.

A great example of the difference between a bend and prebend with release is heard in the song "I'm Bad, I'm Nationwide" by ZZ Top. Around the 0:09 mark, you hear a lick that starts out with a regular bend, followed by a lick with a reverse or prebend and release, and then the first lick again.

Another bending technique common to popular music that you need to familiarize yourself with involves bending a note while keeping another note stationary. In the first measure of Figure 7-20, you bend the D note at the seventh fret of the third string up a whole step to E, while simultaneously fretting the E note at the fifth fret of the second string and keeping it stationary. Because the target note of the bend is E, and the stationary note is also E, the end result is unison pitches. For this reason, these types of bends are called *unison bends*, and a neat tension-and-release sound is created as the pitches come together. After completing the first measure, you move up the neck playing unison bends for other notes in the A-minor pentatonic scale. Watch me in Video Clip 28.

To play this unison bend, most guitarists hold the fifth fret of the second string with the first finger and then do the bend with the third finger, bringing the second finger into play to help push the third string up. You can do the same thing in measure five along the first string, only with your fingers three frets apart to accommodate for the second string's tuning. These last four measures are a stretch, but they get easier as you move up the neck.

Figure 7-20:
Unison
bends.

© John Wiley & Sons, Inc.

Unison bends can be heard in "Green-Eyed Lady" by Sugarloaf, "Spirit in the Sky" by Norman Greenbaum (3:18), "Manic Depression" by Jimi Hendrix (1:17), "Black Diamond" by Kiss (2:37), and the tail end of "Stairway to Heaven" by Led Zeppelin.

Sometimes players hold one note and bend another, and the two pitches are different. Figure 7-21 is based in the D-major pentatonic. You bend E at the ninth fret of the third string up a whole step to F♯ using your third and second fingers while holding A at the tenth fret of the second string stationary with your fourth finger. Some players prefer to play the bend with the second and first fingers; then use either the third or fourth finger to hold the other note. You can try it both ways to find what's most comfortable. Any way you do it, playing a bend like this using a major pentatonic scale has a country flavor to it. Watch me do it in Video Clip 28. Then listen to Lynyrd Skynyrd's "Gimme Three Steps."

Figure 7-21: Playing a country bend.

© John Wiley & Sons, Inc.

Any time you're holding a bend, you can always use a free finger to fret and play another note or notes, whether you play the other note together with the bend or alternate between it and the bend. Additionally, you can bend, bend and release, or prebend all while holding another note or notes. Listen to the very beginning of The James Gang's "Funk #49," the first part of the guitar solo in AC/DC's "You Shook Me All Night Long," and the tail end of Rush's "Working Man" for examples.

The styles of music in which the guitar parts regularly feature bends include blues, rock, and country. A good way to get introduced to bending examples is by learning how to play guitar solos in these genres of music. Think anything by guitarists like B.B. King, Eric Clapton, Jimi Hendrix, Jimmy Page, Eddie Van Halen, James Burton, Vince Gill, Brad Paisley, John Mayer, and Joe Bonamassa. A few specific songs that feature a lot of lead guitar work and all types of bends are "Hotel California" by the Eagles and "Sweet Child o' Mine" by Guns N' Roses. I have videos posted at www.youtube.com/user/GuitarMusicTheoryTab that demonstrate the ins and outs of these solos.

You probably won't hear much or any bending in jazz or acoustic guitar music styles like classical and folk. The heavy-gauge strings used on instruments in these styles of music don't lend well to string bending. The sounds that bends produce don't lend well stylistically either. Incidentally, one of the best songs that serves as a beginner-level introduction to lead guitar playing and bending is Pink Floyd's "Wish You Were Here." The second guitar that comes in at the 0:58 mark features simple pentatonic licks that make good use of hammer-ons, pull-offs, slides, and bends. The tempo is nice and slow, too. But how David Gilmour managed to so easily bend the heavy strings on his acoustic guitar I do not know, especially considering that he plays in a position near the nut where the string tension is most taut. The man must have hands of iron! As for you, play it on an electric guitar or an acoustic with extra-light strings. That's what I do.

Good vibrations: Adding vibrato

Vibrato is a slight fluctuation in pitch, much like the natural, wavering quality of a human singing voice. Guitar players perform vibrato by wiggling fretted notes using a cyclic hand movement. In tablature, vibrato is indicated by a squiggly line above a note, as shown in Figure 7-22. In this example, you play each note twice, first without vibrato, and then with it. During moments of vibrato, move the string in and out of alignment, as if you were doing a series of very slight, very rapid bends.

Figure 7-22: Adding vibrato.

© John Wiley & Sons, Inc.

Because the figure moves through a pentatonic pattern, you can play the first measure with your third finger, the second measure with your first finger, and then the two bends in measures three and four with the same bending technique taught in the last section (that is, use both your third and second fingers to push on the string). The last two measures are doubly difficult because you need to hold each bend in its bent position and add vibrato from there. This means that you wiggle slightly away from the bent position and back to it with rapid succession. Watch how I do it in Video Clip 28.

There are different methods for applying vibrato. Some players, like Eric Clapton, use a push-and-pull motion. Others, like B.B. King, twist their wrists, often in a very exaggerated manner. It takes some experimenting to find the right method, and time to develop the right touch. Plan to develop your vibrato technique over a period of time, not in one sitting.

This next example, in Figure 7-23, gives you an opportunity to put together all the techniques present so far in this chapter including hammer-ons, pull-offs, slides, bends, and vibrato. It's played somewhat in the style of "Hey Joe" by Jimi Hendrix. The tempo is set all the way up at 160 BPM, but I also demonstrate it at 80 BPM in Video Clip 28.

Now that you're familiar with common guitar articulations, it's time to put what you know to good use and hone your chops. Here are some articulation-rich songs that I recommend you look up and learn the riffs and solos from:

- ✔ "Wish You Were Here" by Pink Floyd
- ✔ "Sunshine of Your Love" by Cream
- ✔ "Purple Haze" by Jimi Hendrix
- ✔ "Breakdown" by Tom Petty
- ✔ "Pawn Shop" by Sublime
- ✔ "Yellow Ledbetter" by Pearl Jam

✔ "Maggie May" by Rod Stewart

✔ "Let It Be" by The Beatles

✔ "No Woman No Cry" by Bob Marley

✔ "The Wind Cries Mary" by Jimi Hendrix

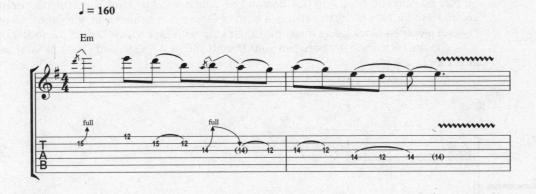

Figure 7-23: Putting it all together.

All these songs make good use of hammer-ons, pull-offs, slides, bends, and vibrato. Though I have focused primarily on pentatonic scales in this chapter, you can apply all the same techniques to major scales, too. A few examples worth trying are the solo sections in "No Rain" by Blind Melon, "Smells Like Teen Spirit" by Nirvana, "Stairway to Heaven" by Led Zeppelin, "Nothing Else Matters" by Metallica, and "Black Magic Woman" by Santana. If you're into Christian music, check out any Lincoln Brewster guitar solo.

Tapping into it

Tapping, also called *finger tapping* or *fretboard tapping,* is a technique where you tap the fingertips on your picking hand onto the fretboard to sound notes. It's basically hammer-ons performed with the picking hand. Although forms of tapping exist in many styles of music, the hard-rock genre is where the technique is best known. The debut of Eddie Van Halen in 1978 is what started the tapping craze, and since then guitarists such as Randy Rhoads, Joe Satriani, and Steve Vai have made it a signature part of their styles.

The first tapping example in Figure 7-24 is one where you bend a note, in this case a fourth interval to a fifth interval in the A-minor pentatonic scale, and hold it up while you tap a higher-pitched note on the same string with a finger on your other hand. In tablature, a note that is tapped with the picking hand is marked with a *T* (in standard notation, a tap is marked with a +). You can tap with any finger on your pick hand, with most players opting for either the first or second finger. Because tapping is usually done only momentarily, many players like to keep a flatpick on hand by cradling it under a finger. This way, they can quickly maneuver it back into position and resume normal picking. With the pick cradled, you need to initially pluck the string in both of Figure 7-24's measures with a thumb or finger. I prefer to pluck using the same finger I tap with (see Video Clip 29). Another option is to grip the pick normally between your thumb and first finger, and then use your second finger for tapping.

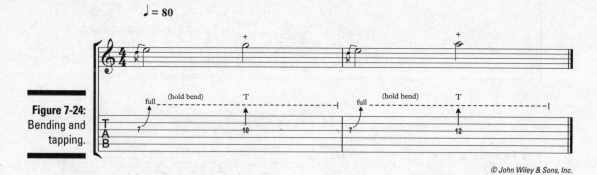

Figure 7-24: Bending and tapping.

© John Wiley & Sons, Inc.

Something similar to Figure 7-24 is done in Pat Benatar's "Heartbreaker" with a bend and hold in F minor at the third fret of the third string, a tap and pull-off at the 11th fret, a bend release, and final tap at the 10th fret.

In Figure 7-24, the tapped notes produce the pitches G and A. But wait, you may say, the taps are at the 10th and 12th frets, which is where the notes F and G are located, not G and A. Yes, but because you're bending the string up a whole step, all the pitches along it are raised a whole step, too. So, the positions of F and G actually produce pitches a whole step higher (G and A). Here's another way to think of it: If you want to tap while holding a bend on the same string, locate your target notes and move backward from them by the same number of steps as the bend.

You see a second tapping example in Figure 7-25 with notes from pentatonic patterns 1 and 2 in A minor stretching between frets five and ten. Before you play it as written, consider how the same part could be played without tapping.

If you placed a capo at the fifth fret of your guitar, you could easily fret the Figure 7-25 notes at the eighth and tenth frets with two fingers on your fretting hand, like your third and first fingers. By pulling off your third finger to your first finger and your first finger to the capoed string all in one continuous motion, you can complete and repeat the triplet pull-off figure. A lick like this is fairly common in the open position, and Eddie Van Halen claims that it was his motivation to move these types of pull-offs around the fretboard without using a capo that led to him getting his right hand involved.

Figure 7-25:
Tapping the
pentatonic
scale.

To play Figure 7-25 without a capo, you need to fret and hold the fifth fret with your first finger and do one of two things:

- ✔ Reach up to the eighth and tenth frets with two fingers from your fretting hand, which is an uncomfortable stretch for most players.
- ✔ Use a finger on your picking hand to tap the note at the tenth fret, an option that, believe it or not, is quite comfortable and efficient for most players.

Here's how the second option, which is my focus in this section, works in steps.

1. **On the first string, fret and hold the fifth fret with your first finger and the eighth fret with either your third or fourth finger.**

   Keep those fingers in place.

2. **Take the tip of one of your picking-hand fingers, and firmly tap it onto the tenth fret of the first string causing the note, D, to sound.**

3. **Pull the tapping finger away in a sideways manner, either pulling down toward the floor or pulling up toward your head, so that you pluck the string and sound the note behind it, C, under your fret hand.**

4. **Perform a pull-off from C to the A under your first finger.**

5. **Repeat the process, being sure to get fingerings in position before you pull off to them, and until you can play the triplet figures back-to-back in a continuous, flowing manner.**

Watch Video Clip 29 for a complete demonstration.

In tablature, a note that is tapped with the picking hand is marked with a *T*. When tapped notes are pulled off to other notes, ties are used just as with ordinary pull-offs. In Figure 7-25, you repeat the triplet figure four times, ending and sustaining on the tapped note at the tenth fret. Then you perform an identical figuration on the second string. Though not shown, you can continue this idea through the rest of the A-minor pentatonic scale. Your fret hand plays notes from pattern 1, and you tap notes from pattern 2. Try it!

Tapping sounds best at fast speeds, which is why Figure 7-25 is played at 160 BPM, but starting at that tempo is difficult. Cut the tempo in half and first work on it at 80 BPM, as I demonstrate in Video Clip 29.

You find that tapping can't produce the same level of volume and the same amount of sustain that regular picking does. For this reason, tapping is aided by increased volume and added distortion, but this in turn creates the potential for more unwanted noise. As a result, the tapping technique requires you to keep idle strings quiet by using parts of both hands to dampen and mute. For example, as you tap on the first string, lay the palm of your picking hand across the unused strings to mute them. When you place your first finger at the fifth fret, position it so that the tip bumps into the second string, cutting off any vibrations.

No discussion of tapping would be complete without mentioning the track that started the whole craze, Van Halen's instrumental guitar solo "Eruption." The highlight of the solo is the rapidly tapped triads that have a classical-like structure. Though the details of the whole "Eruption" performance are beyond the scope of this book, Figure 7-26 is an example played in a similar manner.

Figure 7-26: Tapping triads.

To help illustrate where the tapped notes come from, I first notate each triad as an arpeggiated chord shape on strings one through three; then I follow with the same notes tapped in triplet figures along the second string. You see that this example is drawn from the E-minor scale using the chords Em, C, and D. It sounds best at 160 BPM, but you should cut the tempo in half as you work out the piece, as I demonstrate in Video Clip 29.

In the final tapping example, Figure 7-27, you use multiple fingers on both hands, and all notes are tapped; there are no pull-offs present. This style is called *two-handed tapping*.

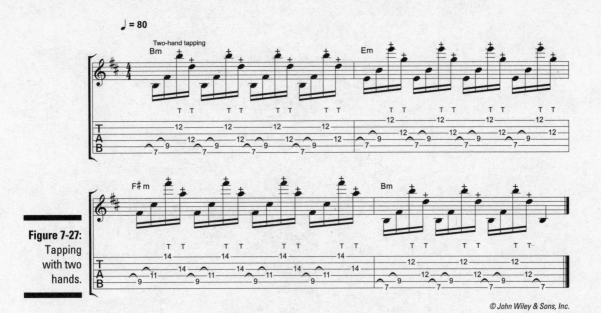

Figure 7-27: Tapping with two hands.

The use of two-handed tapping is very prone to causing unwanted noise, because the open strings ring when you lift your fingers up and your hands aren't positioned in any way that can dampen the strings effectively. For this reason, some players will slip an accessory like the FretWrap from Gruv Gear over the strings down near the nut and out of the way of their target notes, as I do in Video Clip 29. A cheap elastic-core hair tie or a piece of foam or fabric can work just as well to prevent the open strings from producing any noise.

Figure 7-27 is essentially the chord progression Bm-Em-F#m with each chord played in an arpeggiated manner rather than strummed. Additionally, all the chord tones are tapped rather than picked. Two notes from each chord are tapped with the fret hand, and two notes are tapped with the pick hand. I use my fret hand's first and third fingers for the notes in the lower register and my pick hand's second and first fingers for the notes in the upper register. As an example of the way you can vary the part, I also play the part with hands reversed in Video Clip 29.

I play this example using a clean tone, so that you can hear that tapping doesn't always need to be overdriven and aggressive. Joe Satriani's "Midnight" is a great example of two-handed tapping and, like Figure 7-27, is played in the key of B minor using a clean tone.

You start out at just 80 BPM but can work your way up to faster tempos.

Chapter 8

Sounding Harmonics

In This Chapter

▶ Creating harplike sound effects

▶ Producing natural and artificial harmonics

▶ Exploring harmonic tuning methods

▶ Squealin' and squawkin' with pinch harmonics

▶ Access the audio tracks and video clips at www.dummies.com/go/guitarrhythmtechnique

The topic of harmonics is really one of sound waves and science. I'm sparing you the physics and algebra and directing your focus to what guitarists actually do with harmonics on the fretboard. Long story short, you can sound different frequencies on a string by grazing it with your finger at specific points called *nodes*. These harmonics have a distinct timbre, one that is often described as chime-y and bell-like. Harmonics are actually octave overtones, and their frequencies are sometimes higher than the notes you typically hear played on guitar. Because of their unique locations on the fretboard and the ability you have to maintain their resonance, harmonics make it possible for guitarists to play and overlap pitches that regular playing doesn't allow, producing a harplike effect.

Natural-Born Citizens: Playing Natural Harmonics

You can produce harmonics in a variety of ways. To begin, you take a look at the nodes on an open string, which are the locations of what guitarists call *natural harmonics*. The first node you work with is found at the 12th fret. When you play an open string on your guitar, but graze it gently over the 12th fret while in the process, you chime a harmonic that is one octave higher than the open string's frequency.

When I say "graze," I mean just that. You don't fret the string, nor do you press down on it at all. Instead, you very lightly touch it with a fretting-hand finger while your other hand plucks the string in a normal manner. And when I say "over the 12th fret," I mean directly over the fret wire, not the space in between where you would normally place your finger when fretting.

When a harmonic has been produced, immediately remove your fret-hand finger. If you continue to graze the string, then you prevent it from ringing and sustaining properly.

In Figure 8-1 you see harmonics at the 12th frets of all six strings, first played individually, then strummed all together as a chord. Video Clip 30 includes this example along with all the other natural harmonic figures in this section.

Figure 8-1:
Natural
harmonics
at the 12th
fret 1.

© John Wiley & Sons, Inc.

In notation, guitar harmonics are symbolized using diamond shapes. Look at the standard notation in Figure 8-1 and notice that the note heads are not ovals, but diamonds. Additionally, the tab features the fret numbers in angle brackets, which indicates that they aren't fretted in the normal manner.

Like the fretted notes at the 12th fret, the harmonics are exactly one octave higher than the same strings open.

The use of natural harmonics at the 12th fret is widespread throughout guitar music. One of the most famous examples is Led Zeppelin's "Dazed and Confused." In the song's introduction, the first thing you hear from the guitar is harmonics at the 12th fret of strings 2 and 1. Metallica's "Welcome Home (Sanitarium)" uses the same harmonics, only in the reverse order. "Roundabout" by Yes opens with harmonics at the 12th fret of strings six, three, two, and one. Stevie Ray Vaughan played harmonics on these strings in his version of "Little Wing," introducing them at 0:51 (guitars tuned down one half-step to E♭).

Next, in Figure 8-2, you arpeggiate an open E-minor chord, substituting harmonics at the 12th fret for open strings in the second measure. "Nothing Else Matters" by Metallica, which is also in 6/8 time like Figure 8-2, does something similar beginning at 0:27.

Figure 8-2:
Natural
harmonics
at the 12th
fret 2.

© John Wiley & Sons, Inc.

The next node is located at the seventh fret, and you can play natural harmonics across all six strings as shown in Figure 8-3. In this location, the frequencies are an octave higher than the pitches normally played at the same fret. This means that the 7th fret harmonics actually match the pitches you fret at the 19th fret (where, incidentally, the very same harmonic pitches can also be chimed). To help you keep track of the notes, Figure 8-3 features letter names above the standard notation.

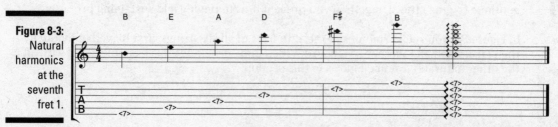

Figure 8-3:
Natural
harmonics
at the
seventh
fret 1.

© John Wiley & Sons, Inc.

Perhaps the most recognizable song that utilizes a harmonic at the seventh fret is Buffalo Springfield's "For What It's Worth." An electric guitar alternates between playing an E harmonic at the 12th fret and a B harmonic at the 7th fret, both on the first string. The verses to Neil Young's "Harvest Moon" feature harmonic runs from the first string to the fifth string, with all harmonics played at the 12th fret except for the last one at the 7th fret. The Yes song mentioned earlier, "Roundabout," features harmonics at the seventh fret once the other instrumentation comes in. Rush's "Red Barchetta" opens with guitar harmonics at the 12th and 7th frets.

Next in Figure 8-4, you use harmonics at the 12th and 7th frets in a manner similar to the opening of U2's "Pride (In the Name of Love)."

Figure 8-4:
Natural harmonics at the 7th fret 2.

© John Wiley & Sons, Inc.

Between the 12th and 7th frets, you find scale tones related to the E-minor/G-major pentatonic. You can ascend this scale starting with an A harmonic at the 12th fret of the fifth string, and ending on an E harmonic at the 12th fret of the first string. As you work your way through the scale, you alternate between harmonics at the 12th and 7th frets (see Figure 8-5). In the second half of the figure, you reverse your direction and descend the scale.

Figure 8-5:
Playing scale tones using harmonics.

© John Wiley & Sons, Inc.

Beginning at 1:07 in his guitar instrumental rendition of "Vincent" based in the key of G, Chet Atkins plays the main melody by starting with a harmonic at the 12th fret of the fourth string, ascending the scale using harmonics in the manner of Figure 8-5, and then ending at the 12th fret of the second string.

If you want to play the E-minor pentatonic scale beginning on E and mostly using harmonics, play an E harmonic at the 12th fret of the sixth string first, follow it with the third string, G, open, then pick up where Figure 8-5 begins. If you want to start on G, then play the open third string, G, first and then pick up the figure from there.

In Figure 8-6, you play harmonics at the next commonly used node, the fifth fret. In this location, the frequencies are two octaves above the open string pitches, or one octave above the harmonics at the 12th fret. If you have a 24-fret guitar, then the pitches at the highest frets match the harmonics at fret 5 (you can chime the same harmonics at the 24th fret, too). You see what I mean when I say that harmonics allow you to play pitches higher than normally heard on guitar. Most guitars don't feature 24 frets, and even when they do, the pitches at the 24th fret are not as conveniently located as the harmonics at the 5th fret.

Figure 8-6:
Natural
harmonics
at the fifth
fret 1.

Led Zeppelin's "Dazed and Confused" initially plays harmonics at the 12th fret, as I mention earlier, but then moves to the 5th fret in the next measure. You also hear fifth-fret harmonics in "Barracuda" by Heart, "Roundabout" by Yes, "Red Barchetta" by Rush, "Dee" by Ozzy Osbourne, and "The Mystical Potato Head Groove Thing" by Joe Satriani. My favorite part of Lynyrd Skynyrd's "Sweet Home Alabama" occurs at 3:08, when the lead guitar plays harmonics at the 7th, 12th and 5th frets, following them with a whammy-bar dip.

Harmonics at the 12th and 5th frets have the same note names as the same strings open. The 12th-fret harmonics are one octave above the open strings, and the 5th-fret harmonics are two octaves above the open strings. Seventh-fret harmonics are an octave higher than the fretted notes in the same fret.

Figure 8-7 combines harmonics at frets 12, 7, and 5. In this example, you essentially play an Em triad inversion at the 12th fret (G–B–E), a Bm triad inversion at the 7th fret (D–F♯–B), and an Em triad inversion again but an octave higher at the 5th fret. You hear the very same thing done in U2's "I Will Follow" beginning at the 2:06 mark (guitars tuned down one half-step to E♭). U2's "Sunday Bloody Sunday," also tuned down, features seventh- and fifth-fret harmonics at 1:19.

Figure 8-7:
Natural
harmonics
at the fifth
fret 2.

Other useful natural harmonics are found at the ninth fret, at the fourth fret, and slightly behind the third fret. In Figure 8-8, you outline an A7 chord by playing natural harmonics along the fifth string. You first play the root, A, at the 12th fret; followed by the major third, C♯, at the 9th fret; the 5th, E, at the 7th fret; the root, A, again but an additional octave higher at the 5th fret; the very same major third from the 9th fret but now at the 4th fret; and finally, a flat seventh, G, located at approximately fret 2.7, which is slightly behind the 3rd fret.

Figure 8-8:
Other
natural
harmonics.

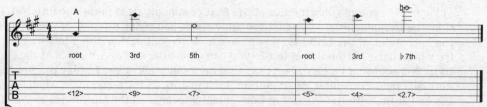

The same intervals from above, 1–3–5–b7, can be played as harmonics on all strings by using the same fret locations. In other words, you can outline a D7 on the D string, a G7 on the G string, and so on. In fact, you can even squeeze out the intervals 1–3–5–b7 by playing harmonics in between frets 5 and 2.7. Just start at the fifth fret and move back slowly from there as you continue to pick the string. You'll hear the pitches change.

The harmonics below the fifth fret are weaker than the others and difficult to hear. You can compensate for this by using an electric guitar at a high volume and with added distortion.

For examples of using harmonics below the fifth fret, listen to the beginning of Joe Satriani's "Summer Song," U2's "In God's Country," and the guitar solo at 4:28 in Rush's "Subdivisions." "Zero" by Smashing Pumpkins features distorted harmonics that are played by slowly dragging a finger along the sixth string from just above the second fret to the fourth fret, picking eighth notes the whole way.

Change Your Tune: Tuning With Harmonics

Before moving on to more ways to produce harmonics on the guitar and use them in music, it's helpful to know how harmonics can keep your guitar in tune. You ought to be familiar with the method of matching open strings and fretted notes at the fifth fret to tune up. You can tune in a similar manner by matching harmonics and open strings. You see three ways to do this in Figure 8-9.

The first section of Figure 8-9, A, matches harmonics at the fifth and seventh frets. The fifth fret of the sixth string produces an E harmonic, the very same frequency as the seventh fret of the fifth string. You can match the fifth and seventh frets like this between all strings except three and two. To work around the second string's special tuning, you match B harmonics at the fourth fret of the third string and the fifth fret of the second string. In sections B and C of Figure 8-9, you match harmonics at the 12th fret to fretted notes on other strings in other positions. There are more tuning and matching possibilities than this, which you can explore on your own.

Figure 8-9: Tuning using natural harmonics.

Artificial Sweeteners: Playing Artificial Harmonics

Guitarists are not limited to only those harmonics that naturally occur at nodes along the open strings. Harmonics can be produced while strings are fretted, too. Doing so allows you to chime harmonics not otherwise accessible. When harmonics are produced in this manner, they're called *artificial harmonics*. There are a few different ways to play artificial harmonics, but before you begin, you revisit a previous figure and play through it using a new technique.

In the previous section, Figure 8-1, you play natural harmonics at the 12th fret by plucking the strings normally with your picking hand, and grazing the strings with a finger on your fretting hand. Another technique that can be applied in the same figure, one that is necessary to play the upcoming artificial harmonic examples, requires you to both pluck and graze a string with your picking hand. This technique is called a *plucked harmonic* or *harp harmonic*. Follow the steps below to properly execute this technique and rework your way through Figure 8-1 again.

1. **Put your pick down and keep your fretting hand out of the way.**

2. **Use your picking hand's index finger to graze the 12th fret of the sixth string.**

3. **While you hold your index finger in place at the 12th fret, use either the thumb or a finger on the same hand to pluck the string.**

4. **Repeat the process on the remaining strings.**

With this technique you do the grazing and plucking all with the same hand. The grazing and plucking come together to form one movement. I suggest you first try using your thumb to pluck because you'll need to do so in some situations, which you discover in a moment. I also suggest that you try using your third and fourth fingers to pluck — they work better sometimes. Remember to quickly remove your grazing finger so as not to prevent the harmonic from sustaining properly. Video Clip 31 includes all the artificial harmonic figures in this section.

The farther away from your grazing finger you pluck, the clearer and louder the harmonic will sound. Reach back with your thumb, third finger, and fourth finger as far as you can.

With your picking hand now holding down both the duties of grazing and plucking, your fretting hand is free to do something else — namely, fret strings on the fretboard. When you barre across the first fret of all six strings using your fretting hand, you raise the pitch of all the strings by one fret, or a semitone. This means that the harmonic node previously found at the 12th fret is now moved a half-step higher to the 13th fret. All the pitches are raised a semitone too.

In Figure 8-10A, you fret and hold the first fret of each string with your fretting hand and then pluck the harmonics an octave higher with your picking hand. Notice the use of "A.H." above the tab line. This indicates that artificial harmonics are in use. Also notice that the standard notation includes both the fretted and harmonic notes. Fretted notes feature regular note heads, and harmonic notes feature diamond note heads. As a reminder to you, the figure includes text explaining that your picking hand is plucking an octave higher than the placement of your fretting hand.

You can barre at any fret and pluck harmonics 12 frets higher. In Figure 8-10B, you barre at the 2nd fret and pluck at the 14th. In Figure 8-10C, your hands are at frets 3 and 15. Continue to work with this exercise on your own by raising the barre and pluck positions until you run out of fretboard.

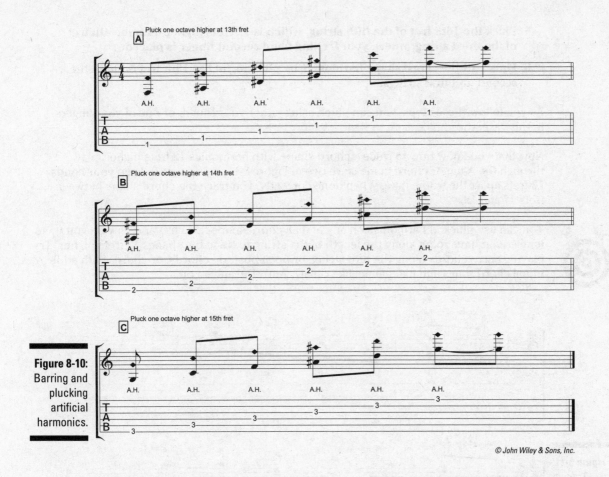

Figure 8-10: Barring and plucking artificial harmonics.

Now that both hands are involved with the harmonic-producing process, you have far more possibilities to explore. For example, you aren't limited to barring all the strings in the same fret — you can hold chord shapes with your fretting hand. In Figure 8-11, you work with standard barre chord shapes on the sixth string, specifically a G-major and A-minor chord.

With your fretting hand holding a chord, use your picking hand to pluck harmonics 12 frets higher on each string. When you do this correctly, your picking hand traces the chord shape your other hand is holding. For example, to play the first chord in Figure 8-11, G, in harmonics, follow the steps below.

1. **Put your hand in the position of a standard E-form barre chord at the third fret, making a G chord.**

2. **Using your picking hand, pluck an artificial harmonic at the 15th fret of the sixth string, which is exactly 12 frets higher than the note you're fretting on the same string with your other hand (3 + 12 = 15).**

   Most guitars have fretboard inlays at the 3rd fret and an octave higher at the 15th fret that can help you keep track of your position.

3. **Working 12 frets above the next note in the chord shape, which is located at the 5th fret of the fifth string, pluck 12 frets higher at the 17th fret (5 + 12 = 17).**

   You should have inlays to guide you here, too.

4. **Pluck the 17th fret of the fourth string, which is 12 frets higher than the 5th fret of the fourth string, where your fretting-hand fourth finger is placed.**

5. Pluck the 16th fret of the fifth string, which is 12 frets higher than the 4th fret of the third string, where your fretting-hand second finger is placed.

6. Finish off the chord shape harmonics by plucking at the 15th fret on both the second and first strings.

As you follow these steps, you can pluck using either your thumb or one of your fingers. In this case, the choice is up to you.

Now that you know how to trace a chord shape with harmonics 12 frets higher, play through the A-minor chord in measure two of Figure 8-11, being sure to keep your hands 12 frets apart the whole time. When done correctly, you trace the chord shape between frets 17 and 19.

You can use plucked harmonics on any and all chord shapes you fret and play on guitar, so long as you have room along the length of the string to trace the shapes 12 frets higher. Try playing barre chords along the fifth string, or open-position chords, or chords with additional chord tones and extensions like Gmaj7, Am7, D9, and so on.

Figure 8-11:
Tracing chord shapes with plucked harmonics.

© John Wiley & Sons, Inc.

In addition to tracing chord shapes with plucked harmonics, you can trace scales as well. In Figure 8-12, you play up and down A-minor pentatonic pattern one (as I teach it) in the 5th position and trace it 12 frets higher with plucked harmonics in the 17th position. Notes fretted at the 5th fret are plucked at the 17th, notes fretted at the 7th fret are plucked at the 19th, and notes fretted at the 8th fret are plucked at the 20th.

You can use this technique on any type of scale, in any key, and in any position or pattern, as long as you have room left on the string to pluck. Try playing A-minor pentatonic pattern two, or a full A-minor scale, or a C-major scale, G-major scale, and so on.

Have you ever thought about playing a riff, solo, or melody using pluck harmonics? Try playing some of the parts from "Wish You Were Here," "Purple Haze," or "My Girl" with plucked harmonics. Chet Atkins uses this trick in his version of "China Town My China Town" beginning at about 0:48. Guitarist Eric Johnson transposes a melody line in his song "East West" up an octave using plucked harmonics beginning at 1:45. What's challenging about his use of the technique is that the melody is played in the 12th position, which puts the harmonics beyond the end of the fretboard. Eric has to trace the pattern over the neck pickup of his guitar! You can watch him do it in his DVD, *From Austin TX.*

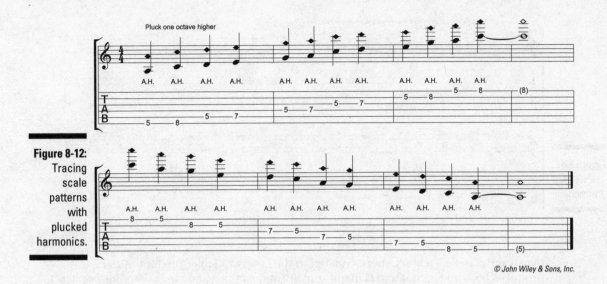

Figure 8-12:
Tracing
scale
patterns
with
plucked
harmonics.

© John Wiley & Sons, Inc.

An alternative to using plucked harmonics is using *tapped harmonics.* Instead of grazing
and plucking a string, simply tap it at the position of the node with a finger on your picking
hand. Tapped harmonics don't sound as clean and loud as plucked harmonics, but they
have a neat sound nonetheless and are fun to play. Try playing a chord shape or scale pattern with tapped instead of plucked harmonics. To hear a great example of what this technique can sound like, listen to the very beginning of Van Halen's "Women in Love."

Playing Harp Harmonics

In the final group of figures, you play parts that combine artificial harmonics with regularly
plucked strings. You get introduced to the full concept of harp harmonics by plucking
everything with your picking hand alone. You use this newfound technique to play through
scales, arpeggiate chords, and create cascading effects.

As you look at Figure 8-13, notice that all the notes at the 12th fret are harmonics, and all
the open strings are played in a normal fashion. The goal here is to play everything using
only your picking hand. This means that you need to not only graze the strings and pluck
the harmonics at the 12th fret using your picking hand, but also pluck the open strings
using the same hand. This is a situation where you must pluck the harmonics with your
thumb so that your hand is positioned properly to allow another finger to pluck the open
strings. When played correctly, your picking hand's first finger grazes all the harmonics,
and you pluck the different strings by alternating your thumb and another finger. Now
you're playing full harp-style! As you play, listen to the way that nearby scale tones ring
over one another creating a harplike sound effect.

In the first two measures of Figure 8-13, you ascend and descend the notes in a scalelike fashion. I suggest that you first focus on getting the feel for one direction at a time; then work
at putting both directions together in a continuous cycle. In the second line of Figure 8-13,
you see a popular pattern that often accompanies this harp-style technique, which is a pattern that reuses the first string as harmonics are continued through to the third and second
strings. In these measures, the notes do not maintain a sequential pattern of scale steps.
Instead, you skip through the scale tones using the high E string as a temporary pedal point.
Harp harmonic users Lenny Breau, Ted Greene, Chet Atkins, and Tommy Emmanuel like to
play this pattern quickly, changing directions and repeating string groups for variation.

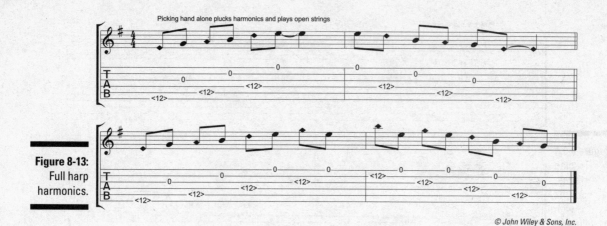

Figure 8-13: Full harp harmonics.

© John Wiley & Sons, Inc.

Because Figure 8-13 features notes related to the E-minor/G-major pentatonic scale, it produces both an E-minor and G-major tonality and can be used along with both scales. In fact, Figure 8-13 sounds as much like a chord as it does a scale, because of the way the notes all sustain and ring together. For this reason, the same harp harmonic idea can be used to embellish chords. When you use the harp pattern in Figure 8-13, it creates an E-minor chord sound with the added chord tones of a fourth and ♭ seventh. Playing the same thing over a G creates the sound of a major chord with the added chord tones of a second and sixth.

Playing harp harmonics in the 12th position is only the beginning. You can raise the open strings by barring with your fretting hand and then create harp sounds for other scales and chords. For example, barre at the 1st fret and harp at the 13th to create F minor and A♭-major tonalities. Barre at the 2nd fret and harp at the 14th to create F♯-minor and A-major tonalities, and so on. Want to create a harp sound while in the key of A minor or C major? Barre at the 5th fret and play variations of the harp pattern at the 17th fret.

In addition to the last suggestion to barre at different frets, you can also hold down full chord shapes with your fretting hand and trace them harp-style. In other words, after plucking a harmonic for each note in a chord shape, follow it with a finger on another string. Most guitarists do this with their plucking thumbs and picking fingers two or three strings apart and alternate thumb, finger, thumb, finger, and so on, with the thumb always plucking a harmonic and the finger plucking a string normally. Revisit Figure 8-11 and play through the G-major and A-minor chord shapes using this alternating harp-style technique; then try other chord shapes and types, including the new ones in the next figure.

When alternating your thumb and finger while plucking harp harmonics, you can create variation by playing patterns that are either two or three strings apart, and by starting with either the harmonic or the regularly plucked string. Additionally, you can play the strings in pairs, simultaneously plucking a harmonic with its alternate string. Try it!

One of the problems with playing harp harmonics on plain major and minor chords is that you produce too many unison pitches. One of the distinct features of a real harp instrument is the ability the player has to strike and sustain neighboring pitches, like a root and second or a seventh and root. For this reason, harp-style guitarists like to use chord types with added chord tones and extensions. You see an example in Figure 8-15. When you follow the D9 harp pattern in the tab, it's as though you play a scale using the degrees ♭7–1–2–3–5♭7. Notice the whole tones. Harping the Gmaj7(add4) produces semitones with the degrees 7–1–3–4–5–7–1–3. You wouldn't normally be able to play and sustain chord voicings like this.

In Figure 8-14, the harp pattern starts with the regularly plucked string. The notes indicated to be artificial harmonics (A.H.) are grazed and plucked 12 frets higher. Watch my example in Video Clip 31.

Figure 8-14: Harping whole tones and semitones.

© John Wiley & Sons, Inc.

In some scores, harp harmonics are indicated using *H.H.*

Figure 8-15 is the last harp-style harmonic example. Here you take it to the next level by incorporating pull-offs, hammer-ons, full scales, and triplet figurations. You begin by focusing on the first measure and following these steps:

1. **Use your first finger to barre strings one, two, three, four, and five at the fifth fret.**

2. **Keeping the barre in place, fret the B at the seventh fret of the first string with either the third or fourth finger of your fretting hand.**

3. **Use your picking hand to pluck a harmonic at the fifth fret of the third string.**

4. **Use a finger on your picking hand to pluck the B note on the first string.**

5. **Pull off from the B note to the A at the fifth fret, which is held down with your barring first finger.**

6. **Use your picking hand to pluck a harmonic at the fifth fret of the fourth string.**

7. **Add a fretting-hand finger to the F at the sixth fret of the second string, and then pluck the string with a finger on your other hand.**

8. **Pull off the F at the sixth fret to the E at the fifth.**

9. **Use your picking hand to pluck a harmonic at the fifth fret of the fifth string.**

10. **Still with your picking hand, use a finger to pick the third string, which is C and completes the scale.**

In measure two of Figure 8-15, you change directions and ascend the C scale. In measure three, you descend again, but this time only using six degrees of the C scale and a repeating triplet figuration. When played quickly, this last measure produces a wonderful cascading effect that is very reminiscent of a harp.

Figure 8-15:
C scale
harp-style.

In a Pinch: Playing Pinch Harmonics

One final harmonic technique to cover in this chapter involves using a pick. A *pinch harmonic* is one where you hold a pick very closely to its picking edge, so close that your finger and thumb rub against the string as you pluck it. Essentially, you pluck and graze the string at the very same time, producing a combination of a primary note and artificial harmonic. This all happens in the area between the neck and the bridge where you normally pick. This technique takes some getting used to — you need to not graze so much that it cuts off the string, or too little that no harmonic is produced. Experiment with your pick placement between the neck and bridge to find a node that will produce a harmonic. Perhaps most important, this technique works best on an electric guitar with a lot of distortion and volume.

In Figure 8-16, I play whole-step bends at the seventh fret of the third string, the kind typically used in A-minor pentatonic. You can tell when to use a pinch harmonic because "P.H." is printed above the tab line and the standard notation features diamond note heads.

Figure 8-16:
Playing
pinch
harmonics.

As you watch Video Clip 32, notice how, in the first measure, I pick the bends normally. In the second measure, I begin to graze the string with the tips of my thumb and finger as I pick, and slowly move from a center position between the neck and bridge toward the neck, exciting different harmonics along the way. I then discontinue the bending and play a phrase in the A-minor pentatonic, using pinch harmonics through to the end.

Pinching the pick and playing harmonics like this produces squeals and squawks that are common to hard rock and heavy metal music. One of the better examples of using pinch harmonics is ZZ Top's "La Grange," specifically the second solo beginning around 2:30. You hear something very similar in Van Halen's "Outta Love Again" at the 1:06 mark (along with just about every other Van Halen song). The more distortion is used, the greater the harmonics scream. For some of the "wildest" examples, check out anything by Zakk Wylde, like "Miracle Man" and "No More Tears," which he recorded with Ozzy Osbourne. Pantera's "Cemetery Gates" opens with a hard and heavy pinch harmonic filled riff.

Chapter 9

Using Alternate Tunings and Playing Slide Guitar

In This Chapter

▶ Using alternate and open tunings

▶ Playing with a glass or metal slide

▶ Access the audio tracks and video clips at www.dummies.com/go/guitarrhythmtechnique

This chapter covers two topics that overlap a bit. The first topic involves changing the tuning of your guitar strings to finger and play chord shapes and voicings that aren't normally possible. The second topic is the technique of using a glass bottle or metal piping on the guitar strings to slide between pitches, a style of playing that often involves tuning your guitar's open strings to a chord. You spend the first half of this chapter playing in alternate tunings without a slide, and the second half playing with a slide.

If you have multiple guitars, it's good to have them on hand for this chapter. Keeping separate guitars in different tunings saves you the trouble of constantly retuning a single instrument.

Using Alternate Tunings

Without getting into all the details behind it, standard tuning allows guitarists to play the most scales and chords possible, and in the most logical and comfortable way possible. Tuning the strings in another manner creates limitations, but along with these limitations come unique advantages, which are preferable in certain situations. For example, because using a slide limits you to fretting notes in straight lines, it's more advantageous to tune your guitar in a manner in which the most usable notes are all in the same fret. In some styles of music, you want certain pitches, ones that are not part of standard tuning, to be available as open strings. Certain types of chord voicings are not possible unless you tune your guitar differently. Some chord fingerings become easier when an alternate tuning is in use.

There are countless ways in which a guitar can be alternatively tuned. In this chapter, I focus on just a handful of examples, ones that are most common to popular music. I have you start by making small changes that don't affect your fingerings much, like tuning all strings up or down a step, or changing only one string. Then you slowly work your way to full open tunings, which require you to rethink and refinger everything that you play.

Tuning up or down

The first type of alternate tunings that you're likely to encounter are ones where the strings are simply tuned a bit higher or lower, with the interval structures between the strings maintained. For example, the most common way to play, apart from standard tuning, is tuning each string down one half-step. This changes strings six through one from E–A–D–G–B–E to E♭–A♭–D♭–G♭–B♭–E♭. (Your tuner may instead display the enharmonic equivalents D♯–G♯–C♯–F♯–A♯–D♯.) This is commonly referred to as *E-flat tuning*.

When tuned to E♭, scale patterns and chord shapes don't change at all — only the pitches change. And guitarists still use the same note positions as standard tuning. In other words, you still call the open sixth string E, even though technically it's tuned to E♭. Likewise, when you finger and fret an open G chord, you still call it G, even though it really sounds like G♭. This is reflected in scores, too. When a guitar piece is played in E♭ tuning, it's indicated at the beginning of the score; then everything is notated as if in standard tuning.

In most group situations when an E♭ tuning is in use, all the guitarists, including the bassist, tune down, so everyone is on the same page. However, when an E♭-tuned guitarist plays with another instrumentalist, like a pianist, problems emerge if pitches aren't referred to in their true sense. In this case, better call an E♭ *E flat* and a G♭ *G flat,* and so on!

E♭ tuning is extremely common. You can't play guitar for very long before coming across it. A few quick examples include "Sweet Child o' Mine" by Guns N' Roses, "Sunday Bloody Sunday" by U2, and "Across the Universe" by The Beatles. Jimi Hendrix frequently used it, including on "All Along the Watchtower," "Little Wing," "Red House," and "Voodoo Child (Slight Return)." Nearly every song by Stevie Ray Vaughan is played in E♭ tuning. If you read my guitar instructional books, you know that I frequently need to specify a song's E♭ tuning.

The reasons for using E♭ tuning over standard tuning are varied. Some musicians just like the lower sound that the half-step difference makes. Singers find that lowering the music a little helps put the highest parts of the vocal melody within reach. Guitarists enjoy the ease of bending that less-taut strings provide.

You may also come across music that features all guitar strings tuned down a whole step, as is the case with "Yesterday" by The Beatles and "Lithium" by Nirvana. "Ramblin' Man" by The Allman Brothers Band is tuned *up* a half-step.

When a guitar needs to be tuned to something other than what is standard, the beginning of a score provides the necessary information. Usually the tuning is marked in the upper-left corner of the music, but sometimes it's written just below the first measure's tab line. Whether to list the open-string notes from low to high or high to low is a matter of preference (or, in some cases, a matter of what your music notation program allows you to do). Be sure to take special notice of on which string a tuning list begins and ends.

Drop D

The next type of tuning that you're likely to encounter is one where the sixth string is dropped a whole step to D, while the remaining strings stay in standard tuning. In this so-called *drop-D tuning,* scale patterns and chord shapes remain the same on strings one through five. It's only when the sixth string is involved that fingerings change.

You get to drop-D tuning by using an electronic tuner, by using relative tuning, or by using your ear. The sixth string, E, is going to be lowered a whole step, which is like moving down two frets if you had frets behind the nut. Most players will play the fourth string, D, open and, while it's still ringing, chime a harmonic at the 12th fret of the sixth string, sustaining both strings while they slowly detune to D until the two pitches match. Some players prefer to simply play the fourth and sixth strings open, not needing the pitches to be the very same frequency, listening for the pitches to sound perfect octaves.

Changing the tension of one string by detuning it can affect others. After the sixth string is tuned to D, check the other strings and make sure that they haven't changed, tuning them to proper pitch if necessary.

When pitches are out of tune with each other, they produce wavering and wobbling sound waves. As pitches come closer to one another, the waves slow down. When pitches are in unison, the waves stop. Keep this in mind as you tune by ear.

Players usually opt for drop-D tuning because of the deep sound of the low D, and the ease of playing power chords. Normally, playing an open-position D chord requires you to skip over and mute the sixth and fifth strings, but in drop D you can strum all six strings. Normally, when you play power chords along the sixth string, the roots are at one fret and the fifths on the next string are two frets higher. In drop D, you can play root-fifth-root simply by barring across strings 6-5-4 all in the same fret and with just one finger.

In Figure 9-1 (Audio Track 40), you play a short example that highlights the ease with which you can play power chords in drop-D tuning. The same figure also highlights how chord shapes that don't include the sixth string are unaffected, and an open D chord can be strummed across all six strings.

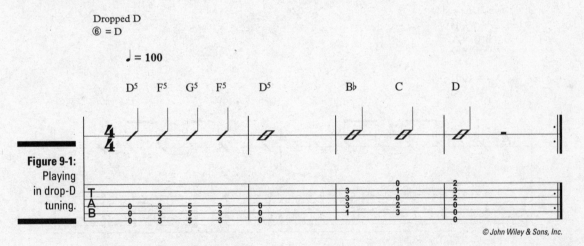

Figure 9-1: Playing in drop-D tuning.

© John Wiley & Sons, Inc.

Drop-D tuning is fairly common. You hear it used on acoustic guitar in the songs "Dear Prudence" by The Beatles, "Harvest Moon" by Neil Young, "Country Road" by James Taylor, and "Your Body Is a Wonderland" by John Mayer. For electric guitar examples listen to "Outshined" by Soundgarden, "The Beautiful People" by Marilyn Manson, "Killing in the Name" by Rage Against the Machine, "Fat Bottomed Girls" by Queen, and "Higher" by Creed. "Moby Dick" by Led Zeppelin is a great example of playing pentatonic-based riffs using a detuned sixth string.

"I Am a Man of Constant Sorrow" by Soggy Bottom Boys is in drop D with a capo at the third fret. "The Chain" by Fleetwood Mac is drop D with a capo at the second fret.

To play Van Halen's "Unchained," you must first tune all strings down a half-step to E♭, and then drop the sixth string a whole step to D♭ from there. Do the same thing for Nirvana's "Heart Shaped Box" and "All Apologies."

Double drop D

This next tuning takes things one step further than the last by dropping both E strings to D. If you're still in drop-D tuning from the previous section, all you need to do is drop the first string a whole step. You can do this using an electronic tuner, or simply matching the first string to the third fret of the second string by ear. After you've detuned both the sixth and first strings, you're in *double drop-D tuning*. Be sure to check the tuning on the remaining strings when you're done and make any necessary adjustments.

In double drop-D tuning, the scale patterns and chord shapes you play on strings two through five remain the same. Only when either one of the E strings is in use do standard fingerings no longer work. Like drop D, double drop-D tuning is typically used in the key of D. There are advantages to having the tonic pitch D always available as an open string.

In Figure 9-2 (Audio Track 41), you play a progression in D using the chord shapes that normally produce Dsus2–Am7–C–G/B. Because the note D is sustaining in the upper voice of each chord, you hear the much richer sound of D5–Am11–Cadd9–G/B. Neil Young's "Cinnamon Girl" does something similar and has many parts that highlight the unique features of double drop D. Young's song with Crosby, Stills & Nash, "Ohio," is double drop D as well and good to learn.

Other good double drop-D songs to learn include "Black Water" by The Doobie Brothers, "Going to California" by Led Zeppelin, and "Gold Dust Woman" by Fleetwood Mac.

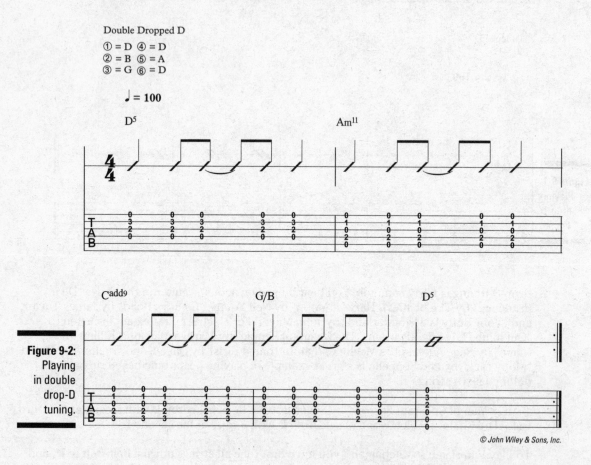

Figure 9-2: Playing in double drop-D tuning.

DADGAD

Pronounced *dad-gad,* this tuning gets its name from the tuning of the strings low to high, 6–5–4–3–2–1, D–A–D–G–A–D. From standard tuning, you drop strings six, two, and one a whole step. If you're still in double drop-D tuning from the preceding section, you only need to drop the second string, which you can match either to the 2nd fret of the third string or to a harmonic at the 12th fret of the fifth string.

DADGAD, which is also called *Dsus4* tuning, has a pipelike sound that is reminiscent of Scottish and Irish music. The best-known examples of it in the rock world are Led Zeppelin's "White Summer/Black Mountain Side" and "Kashmir." Andy McKee's viral YouTube video "Drifting" is in DADGAD. The same tuning is also used on Stephan Stills's "Tree Top Flyer," Paul Simon's "Armistice Day," and Rory Gallagher's "Out on the Western Plain."

Figure 9-3 (Audio Track 42) is an example of how you can play a typical I–V–vi–IV chord progression in the key of D using DADGAD tuning. Notice that my notation program lists the tuning high to low by starting with the first string.

Figure 9-3:
Playing in
DADGAD
tuning.

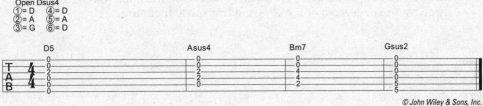

© John Wiley & Sons, Inc.

You could perform a very unique version of "With or Without You" using the Figure 9-3 chords — the song by U2 is in standard tuning but in the same key and with the same chord changes. You can rework any song in the key of D with similar changes using the DADGAD tuning. You can also take songs that use some arrangement of I–V–vi–IV and play them in D using DADGAD, or play them in other keys using a capo. Try it!

Open-E tuning

An "open" tuning is called such because the strings are tuned to an actual chord, usually a major one — you play a chord by playing the strings *open.* In *open E,* you tune the strings to the very same pitches in an open-E chord in standard tuning. If you're still in a tuning from one of the previous sections, get back to standard before moving on.

To get to open-E tuning from standard tuning, first play a basic open E-major chord. You need to change strings five, four, and three to match the pitches under your fingers when playing an open-E chord. To do so, follow these steps:

1. **Tune the fifth string up a whole step from A to B.**

2. **Tune the fourth string up a whole step from D to E.**

3. **Tune the third string up a half-step from G to G♯.**

4. **Check all strings again and make sure that the added tension from the open tuning hasn't put some strings out of tune.**

Whether to use an electronic tuner or some form of relative tuning is up to you. You can find B at the seventh fret of the sixth string, and use it to tune up the fifth string. From there, match strings five and four in a familiar manner at the fifth fret or using seventh- and fifth-fret harmonics. When the fourth string is up a whole step to E, match the third string to its fourth fret. Some people can tune to open E all by ear, picking the strings together as they tune up, listening for the sound of an E chord to come together.

Now that the open strings alone produce a full major chord, you can play major barre chords using just one finger. In Figure 9-4 (Audio Track 43), you use your first finger to barre at the fifth and seventh frets, playing an A chord and B chord along with the E in the open position. You can take advantage of this tuning to play harmonics as well; the natural harmonics at frets 12, 7, and 5 produce major chords in open E. The 12th-fret harmonics are identical to the fretted 12th-fret notes in pitch. The seventh-fret harmonics and fretted notes are an octave apart, but still the same notes nonetheless. The fifth-fret harmonics do not match the fretted fifth fret, however. The nodes at the 5th fret actually produce harmonics that are an octave higher than the 12th fret, so this gives you another E chord, one in an even higher register.

These three chords — E, A, and B — are the basis for all sorts of I–IV–V progressions. Take three-chord songs in E and play them by barring in the open tuning. You can also take three-chord songs from other keys and transpose them to E.

Figure 9-4: Playing in open-E tuning.

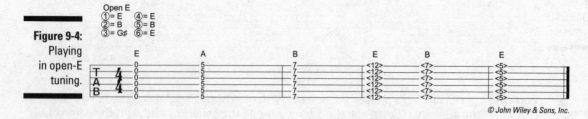

© John Wiley & Sons, Inc.

The next example, in Figure 9-5 (also Audio Track 43), highlights a unique chord voicing for A, and an easy way to make a I–IV chord change using just two fingers. In measure two you take advantage of the open strings to descend the E-major scale in pedal point fashion.

The Black Crowes use the same open-E techniques you see in Figures 9-4 and 9-5 to play their song "She Talks to Angels." I highly recommend that you look up and learn that one.

You can play the E-A chord change in Figure 9-5 in other positions to produce other chords and I–IV movement. For example, barre with your first finger at the fifth fret and then add your second and third fingers to play A–Dadd9/A. Doing the same thing at the seventh fret makes B–Eadd9/B.

Figure 9-5: Playing I–IV chord changes in open-E tuning.

© John Wiley & Sons, Inc.

Open E happens to be one of the better tunings for slide-guitar playing. You take another look at it in the slide section.

Open-G tuning

As I mention earlier, there are countless ways in which a guitar can be alternatively tuned, I'm focusing on only a handful of examples, tunings that occur in popular music with some regularity. This last example has all strings tuned to notes from a G-major chord and so is called *open-G tuning*.

From standard tuning, you get to open G this way:

1. **Tune the fifth string, A, down a whole step to G.**

2. **Tune the first string, E, down a whole step to D.**

3. **Tune the sixth string, E, down a whole step to D, or remove it from your guitar like Keith Richards from the Rolling Stones prefers to do.**

After you double-check all the strings and make sure that they're all in tune, try your hand at Figure 9-6. This example uses the most common open-G chord fingerings, ones that can be played by simply barring with your first finger and then adding fingers two and three for I–IV-type chord changes (not too far off from the open-E chord changes in Figure 9-5). As with any type of open tuning, you can always take advantage of the harmonics at frets 12, 7, and 5. In this case, they make chords G, D, and G again an octave higher.

Notice in Figure 9-6 (Audio Track 44) how you don't use the sixth string. If you have the sixth string tuned down to D, you can play it along with each chord shape and it becomes an alternate bass note. For example, the open G becomes G/D, which is a G chord with the fifth, D, in the bass position. When you add your fingers to play Cadd9/G, the added sixth string makes Cadd9/D, with the alternate bass note, D, being the ninth in the Cadd9 chord. Because this is not the cleanest-sounding chord voicing, most guitar players prefer to leave the sixth string out, or as I mention in my previous list of steps, take it off and use this tuning with only five strings.

Figure 9-6:
Playing in
open-G
tuning.

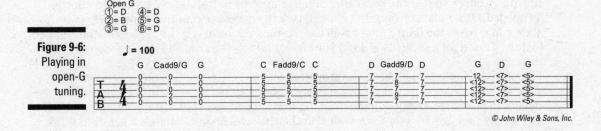

© John Wiley & Sons, Inc.

The guitar player who has popularized open-G tuning more than anyone else is Keith Richards. It's his "standard" tuning and a major part of his signature sound. You hear it in Rolling Stones classics "Honky Tonk Women," "Brown Sugar," and "Start Me Up," among others. Other good examples from the realm of rock include "Twice as Hard" by The Black Crowes, "South City Midnight Lady" by The Doobie Brothers, "Penny for Your Thoughts" by Peter Frampton, and "Dancing Days" and "Black Country Woman" by Led Zeppelin. Ace Frehley used open-G tuning twice on the Kiss album *Unmasked* for the songs "Talk to Me" and "Two Sides of the Coin," tuning down from his regular E♭ for a tuning that is technically, G♭. Open G works well for slide, too, and you take a look at it again, including additional song references, in the next section.

Playing Slide Guitar

Slide is the technique of using a glass bottle or piece of metal piping on the guitar strings to, no surprise, *slide* into, out of, and in between notes. A slide acts like a nut or piece of fret wire, creating a new endpoint from which the strings rest and ring. Because a slide is not actually used to press strings down to the fretboard, but instead glides along top of the strings, it's possible to play *microtones,* which are notes that fall between the semitones (between the frets). For this reason, slide guitar is very expressive and has a vocal-like quality.

For quick reference, listen to Lynyrd Skynyrd's "Free Bird," which may be the most recognizable modern slide guitar recording. After an eight-bar introduction, all the instrumentation kicks in and the main melody you hear is played on an electric guitar using a slide.

Choosing a slide

There are different materials used to make slides, and each material produces a slightly different sound. Materials include glass, brass, stainless steel, chrome, copper, porcelain, and Pyrex. Generally speaking, the more mass (thickness) a slide has, the greater the volume and sustain it produces. Hardness increases the high-end frequencies. Thicker slides work better on acoustic guitars. Because electric guitars are aided by amplification, they can get away with thinner slides.

Ultimately, a choice of slide is a matter of personal preference. You need to experiment with different types of slides to find one that produces a sound you like.

Deciding which finger to wear the slide on

Of equal importance to a slide's sound is its feel and comfort of use. Slides are hollow and worn over a finger on your fretting hand. Slides are worn on the second, third, or fourth finger. (The first finger is not used because you need to have at least one finger available to mute behind the slide and stop unwanted noise.) Some players like to wear the slide on the fourth finger so that the other three fingers are free to fret normal notes and chords as needed. Other players, myself included, lack the necessary control to properly play slide guitar when the fourth finger is in use, so they opt for using the second or third finger instead. How tight a slide fits around your finger affects the control you have over it.

Explore your options and choose a finger that allows you to use the slide to the best of your abilities. Johnny Winter and Tom Petty's Mike Campbell prefer to use their fourth fingers to play slide. Duane Allman used his third finger. Joe Walsh, Bonnie Raitt, and ZZ Top's Billy Gibbons all wear their slides on their second fingers. There's a scene in the guitar documentary *It Might Get Loud* where Jimmy Page, U2's The Edge, and Jack White trade licks on Led Zeppelin's "In My Time of Dying," with each one of them wearing a slide on a different finger.

What matters most is how well you use the slide. Whether you get use out of your other fingers is of secondary importance.

Using a slide properly

After you have a slide in hand and you've chosen a finger on which to wear it, the next steps are positioning it properly on the guitar strings and damping unwanted noise. Good slide technique requires you to:

- ✔ Position the slide perpendicular to the strings, in the same direction as the frets.

- ✔ Target notes by placing the slide directly over the fret wire, not in the spaces between the frets.

- ✔ Push down with enough pressure so that the strings make full contact with the slide, but not so much pressure that the strings contact the frets. You don't want the strings to rattle against the slide or against the frets.

- ✔ Hold the slide level and apply equal pressure across all strings (or at least across the strings on which you're targeting notes).

- ✔ Use a finger or fingers behind the slide to dampen strings, much like you do when performing a bend.

Whether to pluck strings using a flatpick or using your fingers while playing slide is a matter of preference. Joe Walsh uses a pick, Duane Allman used bare fingers, George Harrison palmed his pick while using a slide, Bonnie Raitt plays finger-style using thumb and finger picks. Whatever you choose to do, just be sure to let target strings ring freely and prevent idle strings from making unwanted noise.

Like any type of guitar playing, producing a clean slide sound is a balancing act between your two hands, with various parts of your hands and fingers contributing to damping.

With normal guitar playing, the height of the strings over the fretboard (called the *action*) is set low. Low action makes it easier to fret notes, and prevents depressed strings from going sharp by being pulled too far out of alignment. With slide guitar playing however, low action can cause unwanted buzzing and rattling noise. For this reason, many slide players adjust their guitars (called *setup*) with higher action in order to get the cleanest sound possible. Because slides aren't used to press strings down to the fretboard, there's no risk of pulling the strings sharp. In fact, instruments that are used strictly for slide playing — like dobros, resonator guitars, and in some cases, regular guitars — use a special attachment called an *extension nut,* which raises the strings extra high over the fretboard. Extension nuts work well for slide, but they make fretting with your fingers impossible.

The easiest way to get started with using a slide is by playing Figure 9-7. You know that this part is to be played with a slide because you see the performance note "w/ slide" above the staff and you see lines in the tab instructing you to slide away from the initial notes. To get started, you hold the slide directly over the fret wire in the 12th position, pluck strings two through four, and then slowly slide backward toward the nut, sustaining the strings the whole time as you move. After completing a measure, use your picking hand to mute the strings while you return the slide to its starting position. In measure three, pick the same strings again but this time slowly move the slide up toward the body of the guitar. Follow along with me in Video Clip 33, a clip that features samples of remaining figures in this chapter.

Because you don't outline a defined melody in Figure 9-7, it's really an example of using a slide for a sound effect. You hear this same kind of slide usage at the beginning of U2's "Bullet (The Blue Sky)," only with guitars tuned down a half-step to E♭. Jimi Hendrix's "May This Be Love" and Led Zeppelin's "Whole Lotta Love" also feature slide guitars making this manner of sound effect. You hear Carlos Santana go wild with a slide beginning at the 3:52 mark of his song "Victory Is Won," opting to freely run the slide up and down the strings for dramatic effect rather than focus on any specific notes.

Figure 9-7: Starting easy with a slide.

Generally speaking, slides are used to play melodies and solos, which require more focus on specific notes compared to the last sound effect example. Using a slide is an alternative to normal playing, and an option that gives a part a unique timbre. In order to hear the difference in sound a slide makes, in Figure 9-8, you play a sample melody twice, with the first version of it fretted and played normally and the second version using a slide. Notice that the piece begins with a pickup note on beat 4.

When you get to the end of the first line, the sliding begins, as indicated above the staff with the text "w/ slide." In typical slide fashion, you pick an initial note and slide to another without repicking the string. Notice the use of legato slide ties, with the upward- and downward-pointing lines indicating a sliding movement and the ties indicating that the second note in each group is not to be picked. You can play these same measures without a slide by sliding your fingers from note to note as you fret normally, but the sound is not the same. With normal fretting, you hear the pitch change in half-steps as your fingertip passes from fret to fret. When wearing a slide, you hear all the microtones in between the frets. The slide also produces a different tone than your fingertips produce.

Figure 9-8: Playing a melody using a slide.

When fingering and fretting notes in a normal manner on guitar, all you need to do is place a finger in the proper space and the fret does the work of producing the proper pitch for you. With slide guitar however, extra skill is required to locate notes. Because there is no rut to settle into, you must hold the slide on top of the string in precisely the spot that produces the proper pitch — and knowing when a pitch is in tune requires a skillful ear. It's the same challenge that fretless instrument players face, like violinists and fretless bass players. What's helpful about playing the melody in Figure 9-8 both ways is that you first get to hear the melody notes in proper pitch before trying to slide into them without the help of frets. I recommend that you go back and forth between fretted notes and the same notes played with a slide in order to train your ear to match pitches and train your hand to hold the slide in the right positions.

Tempered tuning

Technically, notes that you fret and play on the guitar are not perfectly in tune. That's because of the way in which frequencies and intonation work. In short, when pitches are tuned perfectly for one key, they're mathematically off a bit for others. It is impossible to place the frets on the guitar so that all notes on the instrument are perfectly in tune in every key. Instead of creating instruments that are perfectly tuned to only one key,

a system called *tempered tuning* is used that slightly compromises pitches so that all keys can be played and sound nearly in tune. Guitars are fretted according to this system. All this to say, a skilled slide player with a great ear for pitch can actually play notes in tune better than a player fretting notes normally because the position of the slide can be adjusted to points just behind and just ahead of the fret where the true pitches lie.

Another nice feature of slide playing is vibrato. By shaking the slide slightly as you hold it in position over a note, you produce a vocal-like wavering effect. Surprisingly, notes often sound more pleasing to the ear when their pitches are blurred through the use of vibrato. Vibrato seems to smooth out the edges in a musically agreeable way.

In Figure 9-9, you see the previous example notated again, but this time with vibrato added to the target notes at the end of each legato slide. To add vibrato, quickly move the slide back and forth in short motions. Don't forget that slide examples are available in Video Clip 33.

Although there is no one way to position and move your hand to add vibrato, most players use the thumb on the back of the guitar neck as their pivot point, then shake or twist the hand to waver the slide over the strings. To get the idea of what the vibrato motion is like, imagine how you would jiggle Jell-O on a plate, shake salt on your food, or stir a drink by rotating the cup in small, circular motions. Don't tense up. Your hand should be completely relaxed and loose. You shouldn't consciously be directing each back-and-forth movement of the slide. When done right, vibrato naturally flows.

Figure 9-9: Playing vibrato using a slide.

© John Wiley & Sons, Inc.

You prepare yourself for playing melodies and solos by first putting your newfound slide skills to use with scale patterns. In Figure 9-10, you play a G major scale along the first string. This is a great exercise because it allows you to practice both half- and whole-step movement. It's a good idea to first fret and play each note normally, so that your ear has a reference pitch. When you have completed the figure, here's a list of helpful things to do next:

- Play the G scale backward.
- Play the G scale on the second string by beginning at the eighth fret.
- Play the G scale an octave lower on the fourth string beginning at the fifth fret.
- Play major scales by starting on other notes, like the A-major scale starting at the fifth fret of the first string, the D-major scale starting at the third fret of the second string, the C-major scale starting at the fifth fret of the third string, and so on.
- Play other types of major and minor scales, including pentatonic scales.

Figure 9-10:
Practicing
scales using
a slide.

Slide guitar parts are fairly common in popular music. The list of songs below all feature a prominent slide guitar melody or solo played in standard tuning, with some selections tuned down a half-step to E♭. I recommend that you look up and learn these parts on your own. Some of the parts are simple enough that you may be able to work them out by ear. When you begin, first play the notes by fretting them regularly. After you map out the positions of the notes, play them with your slide.

- "My Sweet Lord" by George Harrison
- "Give Me Love (Give Me Peace on Earth)" by George Harrison
- "Day After Day" by Badfinger
- "Sister Golden Hair" by America
- "All Along the Watchtower" by Jimi Hendrix
- "Stairway to Heaven" by Led Zeppelin
- "Scar Tissue" by Red Hot Chili Peppers
- "Torn" by Natalie Imbruglia
- "Freebird" by Lynyrd Skynyrd
- "The Long Run" by the Eagles
- "Victim of Love" by the Eagles
- "Running on Empty" by Jackson Browne
- "What Is and What Should Never Be" by Led Zeppelin
- "Tush" by ZZ Top
- "Layla" by Derek and the Dominos

Playing slide guitar in open tunings

In the earlier section on open tunings, you play some chord changes by simply barring with one finger across the strings. For example, in both open-E and open-G tunings you switch to a IV chord by simply barring at the fifth fret, and the V chord is at the seventh fret. In all open tunings, the tonic chord, I, is conveniently available as open strings and also at the 12th fret. Because these tunings put major chords in straight lines across the strings, they're well suited for playing with a slide.

Figure 9-11 requires you to use a guitar tuned to open E (see the previous section). When tuned up, you play I–IV–V–I in the key of E by simply playing the open strings, sliding to the 5th fret, sliding to the 7th fret, and then sliding to the 12th fret.

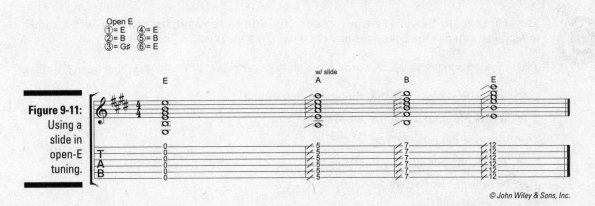

Figure 9-11: Using a slide in open-E tuning.

© John Wiley & Sons, Inc.

When you get the hang of playing Figure 9-11 as written, experiment with playing the chords in new orders. I suggest you play through a 12-bar blues chord progression, like the one heard on Freddy King's "Hide Away." You can play in other keys by starting in a new position with the slide. For example, start with the slide at the second fret for the key of F♯, and play along with Tracy Chapman's "Give Me One Reason" using B at the seventh fret and C♯ at the ninth fret. Don't worry about playing lead lines or any specific parts of these songs; just focus on playing the basic chord changes using the slide in open-E tuning. Use frets 5, 10, and 12 (and also the open strings) to play in the key of A and along with "(I'm Your) Hoochie Coochie Man" by Muddy Waters. Use frets 10, 3, and 5 to play in the key of D and along with "How Blue Can You Get? (Live)" by B.B. King. Any songs that use major chords make good practice, whether or not they have slide in them.

Next, in Figure 9-12 you play some blues-flavored licks in open-E tuning, focusing on the 12th position. The figure begins with a pickup note on beat 4. This pickup note is the fifth of E, B, and is followed by the root, E, at the 12th fret of the first string. Notice how you begin by sliding into the 12th fret on the second string, but you don't slide into the note on the first string. The next phrase is similar, only starting with a slide on the third string, the third of E, G♯, followed by the second string and then the first. In true blues fashion, the music has a shuffle feel. The third measure descends part of the E-minor pentatonic scale. The 11th fret of the third string is the minor third, G natural. Blues players toy with the minor and major thirds by sliding into the minor third first and pushing toward the major third without ever actually landing on it. The tension is released on the tonic pitch, E, at the 12th fret of the fourth string, as you see at the end of the figure.

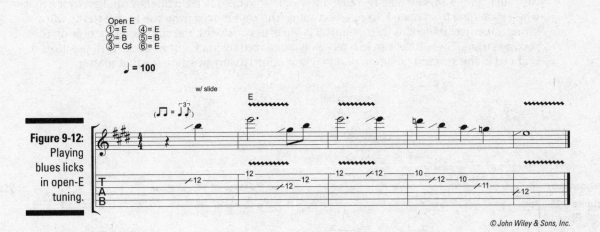

Figure 9-12: Playing blues licks in open-E tuning.

© John Wiley & Sons, Inc.

The licks in Figure 9-12 can be transposed to the fifth and seventh frets to play over A and B. In fact, you can use the licks over any chord at any fret. Try it!

The following songs all feature a prominent slide guitar melody or solo played in open-E tuning:

- "Statesboro Blues" by the Allman Brothers Band
- "Rocky Mountain Way" by Joe Walsh
- "Just Got Paid" by ZZ Top
- "Heartache Tonight" by the Eagles
- "Slow Ride" by Foghat
- "Rag Doll" by Aerosmith
- "The Joker" by Steve Miller Band (tune down a whole step)

Next, in Figure 9-13, you play I–IV–V–I in open-G tuning. Be sure to tune your strings properly before trying it. You can practice playing along with any piece of music in the key of G that uses these three major chords. Van Morrison's "Brown Eyed Girl" and Eric Clapton's "Wonderful Tonight" come to mind. You can also play in other keys by positioning the slide at other frets. Bruce Springsteen's "Born in the U.S.A." can be played using B at the fourth fret and E at the ninth fret, as just one example.

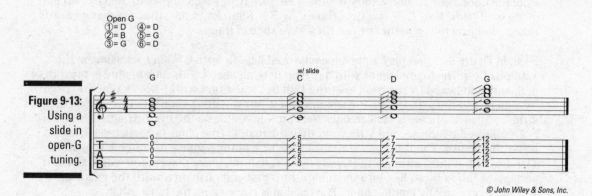

Figure 9-13: Using a slide in open-G tuning.

© John Wiley & Sons, Inc.

Next, in Figure 9-14, you play through a few blues-flavored licks in open-G tuning. Notice that when switching from open-E to open-G tuning, the root moves from the fourth to the third string. Likewise, the major third, on which blues players work the semitones, is now on the second string. These licks can just as easily be played over a C chord in the fifth position, a D chord in the seventh position, or any major chord in any position for that matter.

Figure 9-14: Playing blues licks in open-G tuning.

© John Wiley & Sons, Inc.

This final list features slide guitar songs in open-G tuning. A few of the Bonnie Raitt songs are tuned a half-step or whole step away from G. Be careful about the one up a whole step. Unless you have extra-light gauge strings, the string tension in open A may be too much for your guitar to handle.

- "6th Avenue Heartache" by The Wallflowers
- "Twice as Hard" by The Black Crowes
- "Traveling Riverside Blues" by Led Zeppelin
- "Bad to the Bone" by George Thorogood
- "In My Time of Dying" by Led Zeppelin
- "Midnight Rambler" by The Rolling Stones
- "Love Sneakin' Up on You" by Bonnie Raitt
- "Something to Talk About" by Bonnie Raitt (tune down a half-step to open G♭)
- "Thing Called Love" by Bonnie Raitt (tune up a whole step to open A)

Part IV
Picking-Hand Techniques

Look at The Edge's guitar pick sound in a free article at
www.dummies.com/extras/guitarrhythmandtechnique.

In this part . . .

✔ Practice picking techniques to increase accuracy, efficiency, and speed.

✔ Get folky with fingerpicking.

✔ Jazz things up with chord melody.

✔ Use a tremolo system to dive, dip, and scoop your way in and out of notes.

Chapter 10

Picking and Choosing: Exploring Picking Techniques

In This Chapter

▶ Looking at the ups and downs of picking

▶ Getting to know tremolo, sweep, economy, and crosspicking

▶ Developing picking proficiency

▶ Access the audio tracks and video clips at www.dummies.com/go/guitarrhythmtechnique

Has sloppy picking got you down? Do you wish that you could pick with better consistency and more control? Well, you're in luck, because this chapter focuses on improving your picking technique, including picking accuracy, speed, and efficiency. Don't worry, this isn't a high-intensity training program intended to turn you into a shredder. Instead, I focus on practical concepts that are useful for playing familiar music. You get to know a variety of picking methods including alternate, sweep, economy, cross, and tremolo. You also work with palm muting and string skipping.

Shredding is playing wild, superfast lead lines on guitar. It's most associated with hard-rock and heavy-metal styles of music. Think Van Halen's "Eruption." Guitarists who pioneered and popularized the art of shredding include Ritchie Blackmore, Al Di Meola, Yngwie Malmsteen, John Petrucci, Randy Rhoads, Uli Jon Roth, Steve Vai, and Eddie Van Halen. Michael Angelo Batio currently ranks as the fastest shredder of all time.

Using a Guitar Pick

Before you get into picking anything, you need to familiarize yourself with the proper tools and positioning. Obviously, you need a *plectrum* (also known as a *flatpick* or *pick*). Picks come in a variety of shapes and sizes and are made from a variety of materials. You choose a pick based on how it feels, sounds, and performs. Generally speaking, guitarists like the flexibility of light to medium guitar picks when strumming, and the firmness of medium to heavy picks when picking.

I recommend that you don't use a light guitar pick as you work through this chapter. It's too flimsy to hold up to the demands of the picking exercises you play. A medium to heavy pick will give you more control.

Of all the different pick types on the market, the most popular is the classic Fender Medium. Made from celluloid, this classic pick's shape, size, and sound is a favorite with many players and works well in all styles of music, including for both strumming and picking. It's a good pick for you to use in this chapter. In time, you can experiment with heavier picks, different sizes and shapes, and other materials. There are also picks designed for finger-style playing that fit around the thumb called a *thumbpick,* but these types of picks are better suited for Chapter 11, not this chapter.

Most guitarists hold the pick between their thumb and first finger, but holding it between your thumb and second finger, or thumb and first and second finger, are options, too. The angle of the pick to the strings can vary, but most guitarists do best to position themselves this way:

1. **Hold the pick parallel and at a right angle to the strings, with the pick tip pointing directly at the strings.**

2. **Turn the pick clockwise a slight turn by bending your thumb.**

   This reduces the resistance of the pick against the strings by changing the contact point to along the pick's edge.

3. **Slightly slant the pick so that the top of it (the wide end) leans toward the first string.**

Whether to let unused fingers dangle or curl them up into a fist is a matter of personal preference. One last thing: Strike the strings with just the very tip of the pick to avoid getting it caught in between the strings.

As for the hand position, players tend to rest their hands on the guitars rather than float, when alternate picking is at play. Resting allows you to have more precise control over the pick and puts your hand in position to mute when needed. Place the heel of your hand on the guitar body just above the strings and then move onto the strings and mute as you move across them. Another option is to place the side of your hand in a karate-chop position along the bridge. Most guitarists use a combination of both of these hand positions.

When alternate picking, focus on alternating from the wrist and using only enough movement to cross the string. Your fingers and arm shouldn't contribute to the movement.

Super shredder Michael Angelo Batio doesn't plant his hand on the guitar while alternate picking as most guitarists do. Instead, he reaches over the strings and anchors his picking hand to the guitar body using his free fingers.

Alternating Current: Strict Alternate Picking

This is where it all begins, working on alternating your pick up and down on strings. In this section, you focus on continuous alternate picking — that is, not skipping any downstrokes or upstrokes, and no rests. You begin by using the open sixth string, E. In Figure 10-1, you alternate your pick on the sixth string using various rhythms, including eighth notes, triplets, and sixteenth notes.

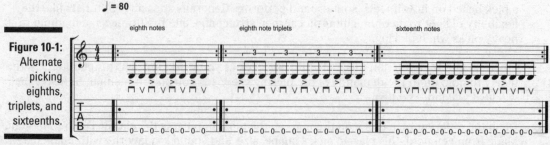

Figure 10-1: Alternate picking eighths, triplets, and sixteenths.

© John Wiley & Sons, Inc.

The first thing I want to point out about Figure 10-1 are the pickstroke symbols under the note heads in the staff. The little symbol under the very first note that looks like a pair of eighths without note heads is a downstroke. The symbol under the second note is an upstroke. What's confusing about these symbols is that the first one looks nothing like a downstroke and the second one, which is an upstroke, actually looks like an arrow pointing down! These symbols are actually borrowed from violin notation and somewhere along the line were, unfortunately, permanently adopted for guitar notation, so you need to get used to them. The figures throughout this chapter feature pickstroke symbols in the first measures in order for you to know the proper pick directions to use. Pay careful attention to them as you begin each example.

Figure 10-1 provides three different rhythms, but you don't need to play them all in order. Instead, work on playing and repeating only eighth notes until you're comfortable doing so. Work on the others individually as well. When you've mastered all the rhythms, you can play through the whole figure as written if you so choose, as I do in Video Clip 34.

In the first bar, you play eighth notes. Aside from playing along with Video Clip 34, you can set your metronome for 80 BPM and practice on your own, continuing the picking for as long as you like. To get started, follow these steps:

1. **Place your hand on either the guitar body or bridge, whichever allows you to comfortably hold the pick in the proper position to pick.**

2. **Work on the alternating action in free time, adjusting your position if need be, and until you can move the pick back and forth across the string in a consistent and controlled manner.**

3. **Set your metronome for 80 BPM and play eighth notes for a minute or so.**

4. **When your eighth notes are steady, move on to triplets and sixteenth notes.**

5. **Over time, work on gradually increasing the BPM and playing at faster tempos.**

The triplet figures in measure two of Figure 10-1 are tricky because you end up alternating downstrokes and upstrokes on the beats, something that requires extra thought and skill. For this reason, you may want to skip ahead to the sixteenth notes before trying the triplets.

You may notice that every note on the beat in Figure 10-1 has a symbol between it and the pickstroke symbol that looks like an angle bracket. This is called an *accent* or *accented note,* and it instructs you to give a note more emphasis. When you pick on the downbeats a little harder, it helps you stay on track and lock into the pulse. From a listening perspective, accents contribute to the groove. With the triplets, these accents are also on the downbeats, but because of the odd-numbered groupings, you end up playing on every other downbeat with an upstroke. In this case, the accents alternate between downstrokes and upstrokes. When you get the feel for this, it's easier than it seems.

I've started you out at 80 BPM, but you're free to adjust the tempo if need be. If the sixteenth notes are too fast for you right now, back off on the tempo until you find a rate you can follow. You can gradually increase the tempo over time as you get better. If you think you're ready for a faster tempo right now, go for it. When it comes to improving your picking skills, you can gradually push yourself to play faster over time, but never at the expense of accuracy and control.

When you get the hang of playing Figure 10-1 on the sixth string, E, you can do the same exercise on the other strings. Try it!

Next in Figure 10-2, you play sixteenth notes on the first string, E, while hitting on the notes of the E-major scale as you work your way up to the 12th fret. Because the scale tones all land on the beats, you accent them with downstrokes that are picked harder than the other pickstrokes. Follow my example in Video Clip 34.

Figure 10-2:
Alternate picking a major scale on one string.

© John Wiley & Sons, Inc.

If it's easier for you, you can start off by playing only the first note in each group of six-teenths, just to rehearse the horizontal scale pattern on the fretboard, and then fill in with the sixteenth notes on the open first string to complete the example. 80 BPM is just a sug-gested starting tempo. You can increase or decrease the rate as needed. When you get this figure down, try the following steps:

1. **Play up the B-major scale on the B string, the G-major scale on the G string, and so on until you play on all six strings.**

2. **Hit the scale tones in some pattern like 1–3, 2–4, 3–5, and so on or try hopping around in random order.**

3. **Play up and down each string using a minor scale.**

4. **If you're playing on an electric guitar, add effects like distortion, reverb, and delay.**

For a great example of how an exercise like Figure 10-2 can be applied in music, listen to the guitar solo in "Let the Praises Ring" by Lincoln Brewster. It starts at 2:49 and is also based in the E-major scale. Iron Maiden's "Wasted Years" does something similar on the same string only using notes from the E-minor scale. AC/DC's "Thunderstruck" opens with an alternate-picked guitar line along the second string that features notes from B Mixolydian mode.

The ups and downs of picking

Generally speaking, guitarists pick and strum down on the downbeat — that is, on the pulse, beats 1, 2, 3, and 4. When playing eighth notes, they either double up on the downs, or pick with the upstroke on the beats in between in the manner of alternate picking. There are, of course, exceptions to every rule, and guitar players are not known to always do things by the book. It's possible to completely flip your picking around by using upstrokes on the downbeats and downstrokes on the upbeats. In his DVD, *Contemporary Improvisation,*

guitarist Pat Bergeson plays turned around like this and mentions that he has always done so and without giving it much thought.

Ultimately, it makes no difference if a note is struck with a downstroke, upstroke, stroke of luck, or stroke of genius. The important thing is to sound notes at their appropriate rhythmic positions in time. What you do is your choice, but in this book I assume you're using downstrokes on the downbeats, like most guitarists.

Another good picking exercise is to practice switching between strings as you alternate, as you see in Figure 10-3. Notice that in the first three bars you begin each new string on a downstroke; then, to mix things up and work on those upstrokes, the next three bars change on upstrokes. You can adjust the tempo as needed and move string to string in whichever order you like. You can also stay on each string for more than just one beat, and try playing triplets and sixteenth notes as well.

Figure 10-3: Alternate picking and changing strings.

© John Wiley & Sons, Inc.

It's important to get used to the feel of accenting both downstrokes and upstrokes, as well as leading with downstrokes and upstrokes as you change notes and strings. I touch on both of these techniques in previous figures. Next, in Figure 10-4, you descend an F-major scale pattern in two ways. In the first two measures, which you can repeat as many times as you like, you begin each new note with a downstroke. In the last two measures, you cut the second occurrence of the F note so that you lead into the other notes with upstrokes. You can apply this exercise to any scale, in any pattern, in any position. Like all figures in the chapter, adjust the tempo as needed and then push yourself to increase the rate over time.

Figure 10-4: Leading with downstrokes and upstrokes.

© John Wiley & Sons, Inc.

Now it's time to move onto playing up and down full-scale patterns, using alternate picking, and picking each note only once. Instead of working your way through an entire pattern beginning to end right out of the gate, I recommend that you practice a small section of it, and then gradually add notes until the whole pattern is complete. Taking this approach allows you to slowly familiarize yourself with every section of the pattern so that you don't stumble when putting the whole thing together.

Here are a few things to notice about Figure 10-5:

- ✔ You play notes from the G-major scale in the open position.

- ✔ There is no tempo, so work at your own pace.

- ✔ The measures are incomplete. Never mind that the measures don't conform to 4/4 time.

- ✔ You see repeat signs. Repeat a section as many times as needed.

- ✔ The figure ends once you reach the third string, but you can continue the exercise until the entire open position has been covered.

Figure 10-5: Alternate picking major-scale patterns.

© John Wiley & Sons, Inc.

This exercise can be applied to any scale, any pattern, in any position. I recommend that you work with more G-major scale patterns, like the ones in *Guitar Theory For Dummies* (Wiley). You can also do the same thing with pentatonic scale patterns. I get you started with A-minor pentatonic in Figure 10-6.

Figure 10-6: Alternate picking pentatonic scale patterns.

© John Wiley & Sons, Inc.

Tremulous Tremolo: Playing Single Notes at High Speeds

When guitarists alternate pick a note at a very fast, unspecified rate, it's called *tremolo picking*. The pickstrokes are not set to specific note values; instead, a player picks as fast as he can steadily maintain. This technique is particularly common in mandolin playing.

In Figure 10-7, you play the open sixth string, E. When you see three slashes below a note, that's your cue to tremolo pick. You tremolo pick for the duration of time equal to the note's value. For example, the very first note is a quarter note, so you quickly alternate your pick during the whole beat. In the second measure you tremolo pick for two beats, and in the third measure you keep it up for the whole measure. Watch my example in Video Clip 34, play through the figure as written, and then practice this exercise on other strings.

Figure 10-7:
Tremolo
picking.

© John Wiley & Sons, Inc.

With tremolo picking, you may find that you settle into a fixed rhythm, like perhaps thirty-second notes, which are twice the rate of sixteenths. You may see some scores that try to notate each and every note in a tremolo-picked line. These things are fine, but keep in mind that, technically, tremolo picking is not a fixed rhythm and doesn't need to be precisely picked or notated.

Next, in Figure 10-8, you use tremolo picking to play a lead line, one based in the double-harmonic minor-scale a la Dick Dale's "Misirlou." I suggest that you play the part without tremolo picking first; just work out the notes and on which parts of the beats they change. When you get a feel for the melody, play it by alternate picking on each note as fast as you comfortably can, and maintaining the picking motion the whole time, even as you change notes. Listen to my example in Video Clip 34. I play this at 100 BPM, but you can adjust the tempo if need be. You can also apply the same idea to other strings.

Figure 10-8:
Tremolo
picking a
melody.

© John Wiley & Sons, Inc.

With tremolo picking, you may find that in order to pick across one string as quickly as possible, you must use a hand position and picking motion that are different from what you use during normal picking. For example, you may float your picking hand rather than anchor it, and you may lock your wrist rather than alternate from it. Experiment with these things and go with whichever options work best for you.

Figure 10-9 is played along the first string and all the way up at the 12th position. Here you use tremolo picking on a melodic idea based on the first five degrees of the E-major scale. Eddie Van Halen does something similar in "Eruption." I play this at 120 BPM, but you can adjust the tempo if need be, and apply the same idea to other strings. This examples is also part of Video Clip 34.

Figure 10-9:
Tremolo
picking Van
Halen–style.

Eddie Van Halen doesn't anchor his picking hand while tremolo picking. Instead, he curls his wrist and floats above the string. Some guitar players refer to this technique as "hummingbird picking" because Eddie's hand floats and alternates rapidly, much like a hummingbird feeding at a flower. You may find this hand position useful, too, especially when tremolo picking along the first string.

In the Palm of Your Hand: Palm Muting

When a guitarist rests the side of his hand across the bridge, and then comes onto the strings just enough to dampen the sound but not cut it off completely, it's called *palm muting.* (Technically, it's palm dampening, not muting, and you use the side of your hand, not the palm.) Typically, this technique is used on the lower-pitched, wound strings, especially when playing power-chord-based songs. "My Best Friend's Girl" by The Cars starts out with a palm-muted guitar. The introduction to "Hold On Loosely" by 38 Special is a good example of a guitar part that mixes sustained and palm-muted notes. "All the Small Things" by Blink 182 opens with strings sustaining loudly, and then things quiet down in the verses through the use of palm muting. "Bombtrack" by Rage Against the Machine opens with a palm-muted guitar riff and Metallica's "For Whom the Bell Tolls" features a palm-muted lead guitar figuration at 1:21.

You can go back and replay any of the previous figures in this chapter using palm muting, perhaps keeping your focus on the lower-pitched strings initially. Be sure to rest your hand near your guitar's bridge in a position that allows you to apply just the right amount of dampening.

The palm-muting position is likely to be different from how you would normally position your hand while picking, so putting the two techniques together will take some reworking and practice. Playing just downstrokes while palm muting isn't so hard, but fully alternating your pick can be a challenge. You may need to reposition your hand, hold the pick a little differently, and change what you do with your unused fingers.

In addition to using previous figures as palm-muting exercises, you can play through Figure 10-10, an example that pedals on the open sixth string as you descend a chromatic line, similar to what you hear in Metallica's "Master of Puppets." You know that you're supposed to palm mute because of the "P.M." above the tab and the dotted line indicating how long to continue the dampening (in this case, the whole time).

Figure 10-10:
Palm
muting.

© John Wiley & Sons, Inc.

To get the most out of this figure, watch my example in Video Clip 34 and then follow these steps:

1. **Play it with all downstrokes.**

2. **Play it using alternate picking.**

3. **Increase the tempo.**

4. **Play it on other strings.**

Clean Sweep: Sweep Picking and Raking

There are moments in guitar playing when you pick through a pattern of notes that features only one note per string and moves directly from string to string in neighboring fashion. You play this way in Figure 10-11, using part of an A-minor arpeggio pattern in the 12th position. Instead of trying to alternate pick these notes as you move across the strings, another option is to use one continuous downstroke to push your way down through all strings three to one. Likewise, you can use one continuous upstroke to pull your way up through the strings in the order of one to three. When you brush across the strings playing notes in this manner, it's called *sweep picking*.

Figure 10-11:
Sweep
arpeggios in
A minor.

© John Wiley & Sons, Inc.

As you begin to play the first measure of Figure 10-11, pick the first note at the 14th fret of the third string with a downstroke; then continue the downward motion as you move to the 13th fret of the second string and the 12th fret of the first string. Notice the downstroke symbols above the tab. Just to clarify, you don't use three separate downstrokes to play the three notes, and you don't strum the notes together like a chord; you use one long down-stroke to sweep across all the three strings, and you fret and release each note one at a time. Start with the first sweep arpeggio in the first measure and repeat it until you get used to the technique; then work with it in reverse using an upstroke in measure two.

In measure three, you add one more note, a high A up at the 17th fret of the first string, which puts two notes on the first string. When ascending in this case, you need to come back with an upstroke and pick the first string again in order to play the last note. When played in reverse, this four-note arpeggio is initially picked using a downstroke before you change pick directions to play the next note on the same string. When you change directions, use the same upstroke to sweep through the second and third strings, completing the pattern. Sweep arpeggios are often played with two notes on the string where you begin and end. Watch my examples in Video Clip 35, and then practice all these variations on your own. You can adjust the tempo if necessary, but be careful not to slow it down so much that you lose the rolling effect of the sweep arpeggio.

Next in Figure 10-12 you move position to position, playing forms of Am and E, sweep-ing as you go. Instead of pausing at the top of the arpeggios, you pull off and immediately change directions. Watch my example in Video Clip 35, and then practice at your own pace, repeating each position and arpeggio as needed. Sweep picking can be used in all styles of music, but it's perhaps most associated with neoclassical metal and players like Yngwie Malmsteen.

Figure 10-12: Sweep arpeggios using Am and E.

© John Wiley & Sons, Inc.

While sweep picking, you may become so focused on the sweeping action that you overlook other techniques. When playing examples like Figure 10-12, be sure that all the notes are fretted and plucked properly, including the notes that you pull off to. The phrases won't sound good and won't flow well if your pull-offs are weak.

While I'm on the topic of sweeping picking, it's a good time to explain a rake. A *rake* is when you push or pull your pick over damped strings on your way to a target note. You see rakes in both directions in Figure 10-13 and Video Clip 35. In the first measure, you brush the pick backward over strings one, two, and three on your way to the seventh fret of the fourth string. This is a signature lick of Stevie Ray Vaughan. You repeat the figuration three times before brushing the pick forward over all but the first string, which you fret and play at the 17th fret, and then slide off. Measure four is a signature lick of B.B. King.

Figure 10-13:
Raking
your way to
target notes.

Using Economy Picking

When you combine the alternate picking from this chapter's first section with the sweep picking in the last section, you get *economy picking*. This type of picking is so named because of its economy of movement. Alternate picking works well most of the time, but in some situations it's more economical to reuse a stroke (usually the downstroke).

The licks in Figure 10-14 are perfect examples of economy picking. Each measure includes a repeating figuration that consists of four sixteenth notes. Taking a look at the first measure, the figuration is based on a D-minor triad. Notice that when you transition from the tenth fret of the second string to the tenth fret of the first string, you pick both notes with downstrokes, rather than alternate. This is a type of sweep and, for most guitarists, is more economical than bypassing the first string so that you can come back at it with an upstroke. Using economy picking like this is especially crucial when playing at fast rates. You do the same thing for B♭ and C arpeggios, creating a sound reminiscent of "Sultans of Swing" by Dire Straits. Watch my example in Video Clip 36.

Next, in Figure 10-15, you move to the key of E minor and play a few different motifs that are typically used in pentatonic-based rock music. Pay attention to the pickstroke directions. Sometimes the need for economy picking isn't apparent until you reach a certain speed, which is why I start slowly and then double the rate. Follow my examples in Video Clip 36.

Next, in Figure 10-16, you see how economy picking can come into play with three-note-per-string scale patterns. Instead of continuously alternating, it's more economical at fast tempos to reuse a downstroke as you change strings. My example is in the key of A major and features a whole pattern that begins in the fifth position. Before you attempt to play through the whole thing, practice connecting each pair of strings using the economy technique, which is how I arranged the figure. I play each measure in Video Clip 36. The same concept can be applied to any three-note-per-string scale pattern, in any key, and in any position.

Figure 10-14: Economy picking.

© John Wiley & Sons, Inc.

Figure 10-15: Economy picking with pentatonic scale licks.

© John Wiley & Sons, Inc.

Figure 10-16:
Economy picking with three-notes-per-string scale patterns.

© John Wiley & Sons, Inc.

Inside and Outside Picking

As you alternate pick passages on guitar, you may notice that some string changes are easier than others. For most people, it's easier to approach a string from the inside than the outside. You need to play through Figure 10-17 in order to grasp this concept. As you look at the tab, notice that the only strings in use are the third and fourth. Imagine that your guitar only has those strings. In the first measure, you pick down on the E note at the second fret of the fourth string, and then up on the open third string, G. As you repeat these notes, your pick always comes at the two strings from the outside, making what's called *outside picking*. The second measure features the same two notes, but in the reverse order. You now pick down on the G and up on the E. In this case, your pick comes at the strings from the inside, making what's called *inside picking*.

Figure 10-17:
Outside and inside picking.

© John Wiley & Sons, Inc.

Figure 10-18 takes the previous example a little further and shows you how outside and inside picking can change from position to position. Notice how in the first measure you need to come from the outside of strings three and four as you change between them. In the second measure, which features the very same notes only in the next position, you change strings on the inside. Both lines use eighth and sixteenth notes so that you can feel the difference that the outside and inside picking makes as your rate increases. When efficiency and speed are of concern, most guitarists opt to play a passage in a manner that allows for inside picking.

Figure 10-18: Outside and inside picking with the pentatonic scale.

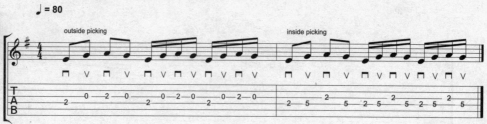

Next, in Figure 10-19, you work with one more example of outside and inside picking, this time in the key of A harmonic minor and using a waltz time signature in 3/4. The two positions I chose have you changing strings with different strokes. As you pick up the pace, what feels more comfortable to you: the first or second line?

Figure 10-19: Outside and inside picking with the harmonic minor scale.

You know from Chapter 6 that you need to use scale fingerings that work well for your fretting hand. Now you know to consider how you can make your picking hand's job easier, too, by arranging your parts in positions that allow for inside picking, if that's what feels best for you.

Shredders (guitarists who play superfast lead lines) like to take advantage of sweeping, economy, and inside picking, in order to play maximum notes with minimal movement.

A Hop, Skip, and a Jump Away: String Skipping

Another technique you want to work on in order to improve your picking proficiency is *string skipping*. This is where you jump over a string or more in the middle of a riff or solo. String skipping occurs when lead lines feature intervallic jumps.

You get started with string skipping in Figure 10-20. In this example, you play a three-note-per-string scale pattern in A major beginning in the fifth position. Rather than play string to string, you focus on playing up and down patterns between two nonadjacent strings, using strict alternate picking as you go. The first measure combines the scale tones on strings six and four. When you get used to this combination, you move onto strings five and three, and finally three and one. Repeat each group as many times as necessary to get used to the skip. When you get used to the exercise, you can apply the same idea to scale patterns in other positions and other keys. I also recommend playing Figure 10-18 in reverse, by starting with the highest-pitched note in each pair of strings and working backward and then back up.

Figure 10-20: String skipping with three-notes-per-string scale patterns.

© John Wiley & Sons, Inc.

String skipping works well for arpeggios, too, as shown in Figure 10-21. These examples are drawn from the key of F using triads for F, B♭, Gm, and Dm. You can apply the same concept to other arpeggios in other keys, too.

Figure 10-21: String skipping with arpeggios.

© John Wiley & Sons, Inc.

In the last example of string skipping (see Figure 10-22), you play a melodic idea in the style of "Sweet Child o' Mine" by Guns N' Roses. In fact, guitarist Slash claims that his now classic riff was originally an exercise in string skipping before band members helped to craft it into a full musical arrangement.

I notate all the string-skipping figures in this section using strict alternate picking, but sometimes you would skip over strings using another picking method. When you watch Slash play the opening to "Sweet Child o' Mine," you see him turn his picking around at times by using upstrokes on downbeats. That seems to feel better to me, too, when I play the song, but I would need to revert to strict alternate picking if the part were set to sixteenth notes.

Figure 10-22: A string-skipping riff.

© John Wiley & Sons, Inc.

Cross Your Fingers: Crosspicking

The final technique related to how guitarists alternate pick is called *crosspicking*. No, it doesn't involve crossing your fingers. With this technique, guitarists use a pick to repeatedly cross over a group of strings, mimicking the finger rolls used by banjo players. Crosspicking typically involves three strings and sixteenth notes played in syncopated figures of three as you see in Figure 10-23 using parts of an open-position C chord. Instead of consisting of strict alternate picking, crosspicking draws from the economy technique, as you see from the pickstrokes printed above the tab line.

Figure 10-23: Cross-picking.

© John Wiley & Sons, Inc.

Guitarists often make use of an open string when using crosspicking, again mimicking the style of the banjo. In Figure 10-24, you see how you can start with an open-C chord shape and move up through a whole scale using sixth intervals while pedaling an open G.

This last example of crosspicking moves away from sixteenth-note syncopation and plays figurations based on triplets in the key of G. The real point of the figure is the sixteenth-note triplets in the second line (see Figure 10-25), but I write it first using eighth-note triplets so you can more easily work out the part.

Crosspicking doesn't always need to have a bluegrass flavor to it. Queensrÿche's "Silent Lucidity" is a good example of the technique used in the rock genre.

Figure 10-24: Cross-picking with sixths.

© John Wiley & Sons, Inc.

Figure 10-25: Cross-picking with triplet figures.

© John Wiley & Sons, Inc.

Chapter 11

Fingerpickin' Good: Exploring Fingerstyle Techniques

In This Chapter

▶ Playing popular fingerpicking patterns

▶ Playing chord melody finger-style arrangements

▶ Using hybrid picking

▶ Using percussive slaps

▶ Access the audio tracks and video clips at www.dummies.com/go/guitarrhythmtechnique

*I*t's probably safe to say that the majority of popular guitar music is played using a pick. But almost all guitar players dump the pick at times to use their picking-hand fingers. In this chapter, I show you some of the most common fingerpicking patterns used in popular music and introduce you to some finger-style techniques such as chord melody. You combine the use of a flatpick with fingerpicking to play a hybrid of both, and make percussive sounds by slapping your hand onto the strings.

Getting to Know Your Fingers

Before you begin with patterns, styles, and techniques, you need to get to know your fingers and how to use them. You focus on using your thumb and first three fingers in this chapter. Classical guitar has a fingering notation system for the plucking hand called *pima*, in which the letters are abbreviations of the Spanish words for each finger (see Figure 11-1):

▶ *p* = *pulgar* (thumb)

▶ *i* = *indice* (first or index finger)

▶ *m* = *medio* (second or middle finger)

▶ *a* = *anular* (third or ring finger)

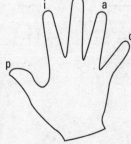

Figure 11-1: The pima fingering notation system.

© John Wiley & Sons, Inc.

In less-traditional settings, you may see thumb and fingers represented as T 1 2 3 4, which is my preference, but my notation program doesn't give me this option so I'm keeping it old school and honoring my Spanish heritage.

The pima system is also sometimes called *pimac,* when the *chico* (pinky finger) is in use.

Guitarists fingerpick using their nails, the fleshy parts of their fingertips, or some combination of the two. In some cases, acrylic or nickel fingerpicks are worn on the fingers. It's not uncommon for professional finger-style players to have some type of fake nails put on in order to keep up with the demand of heavy playing and regular performing. You don't need to do anything drastic in order to work through this chapter, though.

Regarding your thumb, you play with its nail or fleshy part, too. Another option is to wear a thumbpick, but in all the examples you see in the video clips that accompany this chapter, I play with bare fingers and thumb.

Getting Started with Fingerpicking

You begin your foray into finger style by working with a handful of common patterns used in popular music. When you get used to each example as I have it written, you can apply the same idea to other chords, progressions, and songs. You can further explore fingerpicking possibilities by looking up and learning on your own the songs I reference in each section. The further you progress in this chapter, the more likely you are to put together your own finger patterns as you play pieces, which should be your ultimate goal.

Figure 11-2 is where it all begins. You could easily play this example strumming with a pick, and the pattern here is really meant to create a strumming feel by plucking rather than strumming. You can see and hear me play it (along with all the other fingerpicking patterns in this chapter) in Video Clip 37.

Figure 11-2: Finger pattern 1.

© John Wiley & Sons, Inc.

Here are a few things to point out in the figure:

- ✔ It's to be played "w/ fingers," meaning the fingers on your picking hand.
- ✔ Between the staff and tab line are the abbreviated Spanish finger assignments.
- ✔ Bunch your fingers together and have them pluck the strings at the same time.
- ✔ Strike the notes in the rhythm notated, but let everything ring as you do when strumming.

This example is loosely based on the song "Yesterday" by The Beatles, which is a good song to look up and learn in order to further develop this type of finger-style technique. You can claw at other chords in this same manner, by plucking roots with your thumb and some part of the chord with fingers one through three.

In Figure 11-3, you bunch your fingers together and pluck the strings in a manner similar to the last example, but with a fingers/thumb alternating motion that is very similar to how a piano player would alternate right and left hands. Something similar is done in Eric Clapton's "Tears in Heaven," a song that features chords with alternate bass notes just like my example.

Figure 11-3: Finger pattern 2.

© John Wiley & Sons, Inc.

Playing *piano-style* means plucking chord tones all at once in a manner similar to how a pianist sounds chords, instead of brushing the notes in typical guitar fashion.

In Figure 11-4, you use your thumb and fingers independently, arpeggiating chords much in the manner that you use when holding a pick. Notice in this example that your thumb changes strings in order to start chords from their roots, but your fingers stay put. For example, your thumb starts out on the fifth string where the root of the Am chord is, but moves to the sixth string for chords G, F, and E. You can adjust the tempo as needed, switch to sixteenth notes, and change the direction of your fingers, as I demonstrate in Video Clip 37. Led Zeppelin's "Babe I'm Gonna Leave You" uses very similar technique.

Figure 11-4:
Finger
pattern 3.

© John Wiley & Sons, Inc.

No lesson on fingerpicking would be complete without teaching a pattern similar to Led Zeppelin's iconic "Stairway to Heaven," on which Figure 11-5 is based. This example requires that you pluck the first two notes in every measure using your thumb and a finger. After these initial note sets on strings one and four, you arpeggiate strings two, three, and one. Before you try to use the fingering written in the score, see if you can complete the figure using only your thumb and first finger, and then your thumb, first finger, and second finger, as I do in Video Clip 37. With examples like this, there's more than one way to fingerpick.

Figure 11-5:
Finger
pattern 4.

© John Wiley & Sons, Inc.

Figure 11-6 features one of the most commonly used fingerpicking patterns in all of music. It has a folk influence, so variations of it are used in familiar acoustic guitar songs such as "Landslide" by Fleetwood Mac, "Dust in the Wind" by Kansas, and "One Too Many Mornings" by Bob Dylan. Before you try to tackle the whole thing, focus only on the C chord in the first measure.

Finger pattern 5 can be broken down easily into the following movements:

1. Thumb and second finger together

2. Thumb then first finger separately

3. Thumb then second finger separately

4. Thumb

Your thumb moves back and forth between strings five and four with each step. Your first and second fingers stay on their respective strings.

Practice only the first measure of Figure 11-6 until your fingers get used to the pattern on the C chord and you play it by feel rather than thinking about the steps. When you work out the pattern on the G chord in the third measure, you notice that your thumb starts out on the sixth string where the root of the G chord lies, but all the other strings are picked the same. Your finger placements on chords C and Am remain the same. With the F chord, you work the pattern between strings one through four, thus starting your thumb on F at the third fret of the fourth string. Only when you work the pattern individually on all four chords should you attempt to put the whole progression together, repeating each measure as the repeat signs instruct you to do.

Figure 11-6: Finger pattern 5.

© John Wiley & Sons, Inc.

When you feel up to it, try doubling the rate and playing the pattern with sixteenth notes as I do in Video Clip 37.

In folk-influenced music, finger patterns are often played on chords that use fifths as alternate bass notes. In the previous example, your thumb alternates between strings within each chord shape, but in Figure 11-7 you actually add a bass note to the lower voicing of each chord. Like the previous example, work out each chord slowly and one at a time before you attempt to put the whole progression together.

Here are a few things to note about Figure 11-7:

- Your fretting-hand's third finger will move back and forth between the C at the third fret of the fifth string and the alternate bass note, G, at the third fret of the sixth string, or you can use your third and fourth fingers to fret both.

- Your thumb plays the strings 5–4–6–4, 5–4–6–4, and so on, and it's a good idea to rehearse this movement by itself as a first step.

- Aside from the preceding two points, the C-chord pattern remains the same as the previous figure.

- The F chord works just like the C chord, but with everything moved over and played between strings one through five, with the alternate bass note, now C, at the third fret of the fifth string.

- The G chord actually alternates to a fifth in the middle voicing of the chord. In order to leave the D string available for this purpose, play the pattern using strings one, two, three, and six, with the fourth string serving as the alternate bass note. This means that your thumb plays the strings 6–3–4–3, 6–3–4–3, and so on.

- The figure sounds better when played as sixteenth notes, as I demonstrate in Video Clip 37.

Figure 11-7: Finger pattern 6.

© John Wiley & Sons, Inc.

Figure 11-8 is a version of the folk pattern in Figure 11-6 that features melodic movement in the upper register similar to Elizabeth Cotten's "Freight Train." Compared to Figure 11-6, this pattern uses an additional string, the first string, which features part of the melody. You can either go back and forth between strings two and one with your second finger as needed, or bring your third finger into play on the first string. I don't include fingerings in Figure 11-8, so how you approach it is your call.

Figure 11-8: Finger pattern 7.

© John Wiley & Sons, Inc.

PLAY THIS!

Listen to my example in Video Clip 37 and try if you're able to play using both eighth and sixteenth notes, adjusting your tempo as needed.

Playing Chord Melody Style

When a guitarist arranges a song's main melody and chords together to form one part, it's called playing — big surprise — *chord melody*. You're introduced to chord melody a bit in Figure 11-8, but now in Figure 11-9 it becomes the main focus. For this example, you play a version of the popular Christmas carol, "What Child Is This?," which is an adaptation of an earlier folksong, "Greensleeves."

Figure 11-9: Playing chord melody on "What Child Is This?"

Figure 11-9:
(continued)

Before you try to play the arrangement in Figure 11-9 as written, I suggest you take a moment to familiarize yourself with the melody. The melody is voice 1 in the score and features note stems that go up. Watch my demonstration in Video Clip 38, pay attention to the 3/4 waltz time, and then work out the melody on your own, ignoring for now voice 2 in the score, which features note stems going down. When you're familiar with the main melody, you're ready to add in the other elements of the arrangement.

Figure 11-9 has two sections, A and B, and each one is played in two different manners. Here's a list of what each section includes:

✔ In section A1, you begin to build a chord melody arrangement by adding the root note from each chord using your thumb as you play through the melody with your fingers.

✔ In section A2, you fill the space between the bass note and melody by using your fingers to pluck parts of each chord piano-style.

✔ In the first half of the song's B section, you continue to pluck piano-style but with a twist. Instead of plucking the strings all at once, use a forward roll that begins with the bass note and ends with the melody note. Watch my demonstration in Video Clip 38 to hear how this technique should sound.

✔ Finally in B2, you fill the space between the bass and melody notes with arpeggiation.

I suggest that you work on only one approach from this list at a time. When you get a technique down, apply it through the entire tune. In other words, the whole piece can be played using root notes from each chord as they change, as described in the first step. Likewise the whole piece can be played piano-style, or with forward rolls, or with arpeggiation. When you're really good, you use a mixture of all four styles and pick and choose how to approach each chord as you play.

You can adapt a tune for chord melody by putting the lead line in the upper voicing of the chords.

Chord-melody-style guitar is more common in jazz than in pop/rock, and getting into all its intricacies is beyond the scope of this book, but just to whet your appetite, I include a jazzy example in Figure 11-10 played somewhat in the style of Vince Guaraldi Trio's "O Tannenbaum" from the soundtrack, *A Charlie Brown Christmas*. Notice that the melody is voice 1 in the score with the stems going up, and played mostly on the first string. I don't include a specific fingering. You can use whatever feels right and works. If you have trouble getting to the Bm7 in measure four, try omitting one of the strings to make it easier. Watch my demonstration in Video Clip 38.

Figure 11-10: Playing chord melody in the style of Vince Guaraldi.

Hybrid Picking: Using a Pick and Fingers

When a guitarist's approach to playing includes flatpicking and fingerpicking simultaneously, it's called *hybrid picking*. This is accomplished by holding a pick in the conventional way, and then using your remaining fingers to pluck as well. One way to get started with this is by playing chords piano-style as you do in Figure 11-11. In this example, you pick the roots of each chord with the pick, and pluck the other two chord tones with your second and third fingers (*medio* and *anular*). Notice the fingerings above the tab line plus the use of a down pickstroke symbol.

Figure 11-11: Hybrid picking in the style of Eric Johnson.

© John Wiley & Sons, Inc.

Hybrid picking like this is a favorite technique of guitarist Eric Johnson, who plays unique chord voicings by skipping strings and even getting his picking-hand pinky involved at times, usually using a sparkling clean tone with added digital delay. Watch my demonstration in Video Clip 39.

Next, in Figure 11-12, you get both your pick and fingers involved again to play some typical country- and rockabilly-style *double-stops* (two-note groups). In this example, all the lone notes are played using your pick, and the *double-stops* are played using your second and third fingers (*medio* and *anular*) on your picking hand. To have added fun with this lick, move from A in the 5th position up to D in the 10th position and E in the 12th position, which are the I–IV–V chords used in a standard 12-bar blues chord progression. Watch my example in Video Clip 39.

Figure 11-12: Using country-style hybrid picking.

© John Wiley & Sons, Inc.

No lesson on hybrid picking would be complete without a twangy, country guitar example. Figure 11-13 features a classic country double-stop bend followed by a major blues scale run with combined picked and plucked notes. The open bend at the fourth fret of the third string should be played along with the fifth fret of the second string, which is not to be bent. As you hold the double-stop bend in position, use your picking hand's second and third fingers (*medio* and *anular*) to pluck the strings, cutting the strings off after each strike (called a *choke*). The bend is not released until beat three. Notice that you use your picking hand's second finger to pluck two notes in the run that follows, too. Pay close attention to the pick-hand fingerings written above the tab.

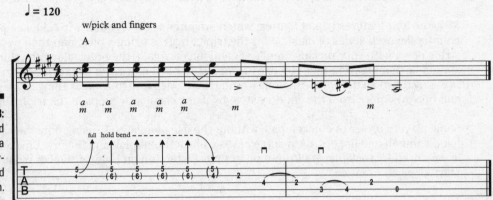

Figure 11-13: Hybrid picking a country-style bend and run.

In order to get the snappy sound that is indicative of country music, the fingerpicked notes need to really pop, so pluck them hard and watch my example in Video Clip 39.

This last hybrid picking example, Figure 11-14 (Video Clip 39), kills two birds with one stone, so to speak. Like the previous examples, you use a combination of a pick and your finger, but with the addition of damped notes and string popping. The end result is a sound known in guitarland as *chicken pickin'*, a distinctive technique in the country-music genre with players such as James Burton, Albert Lee, Brent Mason, and Brad Paisley. Chicken pickin' is said to emulate the sound of a chicken clucking.

Figure 11-14: Using chicken pickin'.

Figure 11-14 features the use of sixths beginning with E major in the 12th position and moving backward down the dominant scale (also known as *Mixolydian mode*). The first measure is played normally, and by using your pick on the third string and your picking hand's second finger on the first string. The second measure is where the chicken pickin' effect begins to take shape. The notes along the third string should be damped (hence, the palm-mute indications above the tab). The notes on the first string should be played staccato by snapping (or *popping*) them with your picking-hand finger and quickly cutting them off by releasing your fretting-hand finger. As an alternative to palm muting, you can dampen the notes on the third string by not fretting them all the way. When notes are fretted but not completely depressed to the fretboard, they're sometimes notated as X's as you see in measure three.

Measure four features triplet figures, which are often used together with chicken pickin' in country-flavored styles of music. Play the triplet figures using a pick, and then pop the first string notes with your picking hand's second finger. Again, the notes along the third string should be damped, whether you use picking-hand palm muting or the technique of not pressing down all the way with your fretting hand. Measure four takes things a step further and borrows more from the country style by using chromatic steps in the triplet figures.

Some players prefer to chicken-pick without the use of a flatpick, using only their picking hand's thumb and fingers, or in some cases using a thumbpick and fingers. Chicken pickin' is employed by rock players from time to time. Listen to Van Halen's "Finish What You Started" as an example.

Slap Happy: Incorporating Slap Rhythm into Your Playing

The final finger-style technique you familiarize yourself with in this chapter is the practice of slapping the strings to play notes or produce percussive sounds. Slapping can take on many forms and include a variety of techniques, and is especially prevalent in bass-guitar playing, but my examples focus only on a few practical applications in guitar playing.

Figure 11-15 reprises a bit of Figure 11-2 by using your fingers in a bunch formation and breaking up chords into bass notes and remaining chord tones. The muted notes on beats two and four are when the slapping comes into play. At these points, slap your hand onto the strings, holding it down enough to completely cut off the strings. Whether to use an open or closed hand is up to you — I recommend that you try it both ways. You'll probably need to learn this example in chunks, stopping to rehearse small sections until you coordinate the movements. When you get it all together, the slaps hit the backbeats (two and four) just like a drummer hits a snare when playing a drum beat, and this percussive example is a knockoff (so to speak) of Extreme's "More Than Words." This example is part of Video Clip 40.

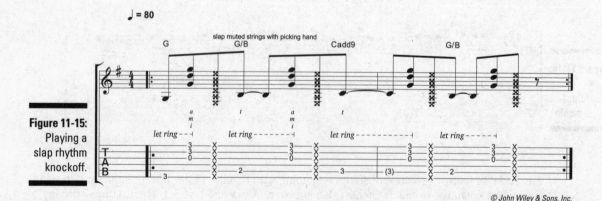

Figure 11-15: Playing a slap rhythm knockoff.

You reprise a bit of Figure 11-4 to play Figure 11-16 by using forward finger rolls. Here you play chord shapes based on E-form barre chords. I like to wrap my left-hand thumb around the neck and use it to fret the root notes on the sixth string a la "Hendrix-style." In fact, there's no other way to play the Gsus2. Each finger roll is followed by a slap and then, as an added percussive element, two muted notes on strings six and four a la guitarist Ben Lacy. These muted notes are played by plucking the strings with your thumb and first finger while your fretting-hand damps the strings. You may find it best to work this figure out in steps by focusing on the fretted notes first, then adding the slaps, then adding the extra muted notes. You see me put it all together in Video Clip 40.

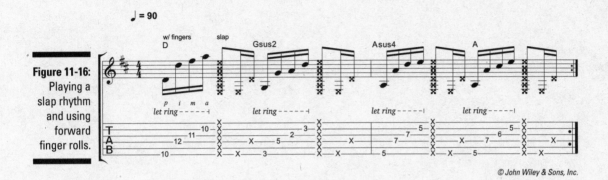

Figure 11-16: Playing a slap rhythm and using forward finger rolls.

© John Wiley & Sons, Inc.

Figure 11-17 is the final slap example and includes a few new features. It's presented in pieces so that you work your way up to the whole thing step by step. First off, you play a scale riff in the style of "My Girl" by The Temptations. Next you add a slap on beat two. In the third measure, you add a slap on beat four, but that's not all. The slaps on the backbeats are used to sound pitches, namely G, C, and E from the C chord, and A in the riff. I don't include fingerings here — you're on your own to decide what works best.

Figure 11-17: Slapping with your thumb.

© John Wiley & Sons, Inc.

Using slaps to sound notes introduces new challenges. First, you need to target specific strings more precisely. Second, you need to mute the strings around the notes that you target. In this type of situation, guitarists usually opt to slap with the side of the thumb, much in the same way that bass players do, and use fingers on the fret-hand to keep idle strings from ringing. With practice, and by adjusting the angle of your thumb, you can sound groups of notes on multiple strings, and single notes on one string.

When you manage to get a handle on measure three in Figure 11-17, you transpose the part to F. From there, you can repeat the C and F measures, much like the song "My Girl" does. This example is also part of Video Clip 40.

John Mayer is especially skilled at using slaps and muted notes in his rhythm guitar parts, even going so far as to play thumb slaps and finger flicks simultaneously to sound notes and produce percussive hits at the same time. You hear him do this in his songs "Why Georgia," "The Heart of Life," "Stop This Train," "Who Says," and even his live version of "Your Body Is a Wonderland" as performed at the 2003 Grammy Awards.

Chapter 12

Using a Tremolo System

*I*n this chapter, I introduce you to techniques involving the bars attached to spring-loaded guitar bridges. These techniques include vibrato, diving, dipping, and scooping. These techniques create interesting sounds and add to the guitar's expressive capabilities.

Obviously, in order to follow along with this chapter, you need a tremolo-equipped guitar, and the system needs to be operational. Make sure that you're comfortably able to depress the bar and that the bridge returns to its resting position with strings in pitch. If you aren't familiar with tremolo systems, see the nearby sidebar, "Tremolo 101," before you start.

Defining Tremolo

Tremolo refers to volume fluctuation. Think about how the guitar's volume in "Crimson and Clover" by Tommy James and the Shondells fluctuates in a pulsating manner. *Tremolo picking* refers to the technique of rapidly repeating a note, the way Dick Dale does. You see more on tremolo picking in Chapter 10.

Technically speaking, the bars connected to spring-loaded guitar bridges produce vibrato because they're used to fluctuate the pitch of the strings. Likewise, the circuitry in amplifiers that pulsate the volume produce a tremolo effect. But here's where things get weird. In the early days of electric-guitar design and amplifier manufacturing, the two terms (*vibrato* and *tremolo*) somehow got crossed, resulting in the spring-loaded and bar-equipped bridge systems being called *tremolo systems* and the volume-pulsating circuitry being called *vibrato.* For example, think about Fender's synchronized tremolo, which debuted on the Stratocaster back in 1954 and still endures in various forms to this day. Or think about the introduction of Fender's Vibroverb, Vibrosonic Reverb, and Vibro Champ amps in the 1960s.

Similar to the fall of man as recorded in *Genesis,* the vibrato/tremolo debacle has corrupted the once-good state of guitar vernacular. There's no chance for salvation in this case, though — guitarists need to live with it. From here on out in this chapter, my use of the word *tremolo* or *trem* refers to the bridge systems that produce vibrato.

Want to be even more confused? You sometimes hear a tremolo system referred to as a whammy bar. The name *whammy bar* is inspired by the 1963 guitar instrumental, "Wham!" The song features use of guitarist Lonnie Mack's tremolo-system-equipped Gibson Flying V. So, whammy bar, vibrato bar, tremolo arm, trem bar, wiggle stick, twang bar . . . whatever you call it, it refers to the pieces of hardware sticking out from guitar bridges that guitarists push and pull on to raise and lower the pitch of strings and add vibrato.

Tremolo 101

Spring-loaded tremolo systems fit onto guitars in two basic ways. Either the spring mechanism is mounted on top of the body (as is the case with the Bigsby vibrato tailpiece) or it rests in a routed-out cavity underneath the bridge (as is the case with the Fender synchronized tremolo). The tension of the trem arm is adjusted by tightening and loosening the springs or, in some cases, adding and removing springs. Systems where the bridge rests in an in-between position that allows you to both push down and pull up on the bar are called *floating tremolos*.

The change in tension that the strings go through with extreme trem bar usage can cause the wrappings around the tuning posts to loosen or tighten, throwing a guitar's tuning out of whack. In order to prevent string slippage from putting a guitar out of tune, some systems, like the Floyd Rose locking tremolo, also feature a locking nut or locking tuners. A locking nut has little clamps that press down on the strings as they pass through the

nut, preventing any slipping on the tuning pegs. With locking tuners, the strings are clamped at the tuning pegs and string windings are eliminated.

Some tremolo systems feature threaded trem arms that screw into place. As the bars are screwed in, they eventually tighten completely and come to rest in some position, one that may not be where you prefer the bar to be. When they're not screwed in all the way, they often dangle loosely and just out of reach. If you can't get the trem arm to rest in a convenient position, try wrapping the threads in plumber's tape (the Teflon kind) before screwing it in. By adjusting the amount of tape you use, you can get the bar to rest in just the right position for you, and even keep the bar in place without needing to screw it down tightly. A tremolo system that features a bar without threads usually has a tiny hex screw that's used to adjust the bar's rotary tension and help keep it in a preferred fixed position.

Using a Tremolo System

A tremolo system is a spring-loaded bridge that allows you to push and pull on a bar to lower and raise the pitch of the strings. The tension of the strings is balanced against springs that pull the strings back into proper pitch when the pressure on the bar is released. Aside from the obvious — adding vibrato — you use the trem bar to both dive away from and scoop up to pitches. These techniques add to the guitar's expressive capabilities.

The use of tremolo systems ranges from subtle to extreme. Think about Stevie Ray Vaughan's jazz-inflected vibrato-bar use in "Lenny" and "Riviera Paradise." On the other end of the spectrum, think about the dive bombs in Jimi Hendrix's performance of the "The Star-Spangled Banner" at Woodstock and Eddie Van Halen's "Eruption." Somewhere in the middle, you find Jeff Beck, who bends in and out of notes using the trem arm, conjuring up a fairly convincing slide sound. Although there are all sorts of whammy-bar tricks and noises to be played and heard, this chapter focuses on the basics, those techniques that are most common in and most useful for playing popular music.

Trem-bar vibrato

The first and most obvious use of a tremolo system involves using it to add vibrato to a note or chord. In Figure 12-1, you play a couple notes related to A minor — the root A and the third C. In order to get the idea of how trem-bar vibrato works, I have you alternate between playing each note without vibrato and with vibrato. Additionally, you alternate between finger vibrato (see Chapter 7) and trem-bar vibrato. In the notation, notice the vibrato lines above every other note. Notice the difference in vibrato lines, and the mention of "w/ trem. bar." Work toward making your trem-bar vibrato as smooth as your finger vibrato.

All examples in this chapter can be seen in Video Clip 41.

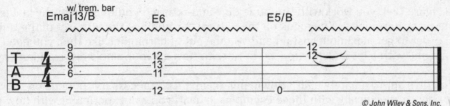

Figure 12-1:
Adding
trem-bar
vibrato to
notes.

© John Wiley & Sons, Inc.

Next, in Figure 12-2 , you add trem-bar vibrato to chords, playing in the style of Stevie Ray Vaughan's "Lenny." You hear the same technique used in "Riviera Paradise" by Stevie Ray Vaughan, "Country Gentleman" by Chet Atkins, and "Sleepwalk" by Brian Setzer.

Figure 12-2:
Adding
trem-bar
vibrato to
chords.

© John Wiley & Sons, Inc.

You vary the amount of vibrato by how quickly you move the trem bar and how far you push and pull.

Trem-bar dive

Apart from adding vibrato, trem bars are used to lower the pitch of notes. This movement is called a *dive* and can be shallow or deep, depending on whether a player wants to be subtle or dramatic. When you hear a trem-bar dive return a note to its original pitch, it's called a *dive and return*. Sometimes players dive on one note and return on another.

In Figure 12-3 you use the open sixth string, E, to play common trem-bar dive variations. Notice that the notation instructs you to play these parts "w/ trem. bar." The downward- and upward-leaning lines above the tab represent the down-and-up motion of your trem bar. The number by these lines indicates how far the pitch should drop — in this case, a fifth, but that's only an approximation for these examples, and you don't need to worry about diving to a specific pitch right now.

Here's how all four measures break down:

- ✔ **In the first measure, you strike the string, push down on the trem bar to lower the pitch, and then cut the string off so that it no longer sustains.** This technique can be done on any note, open string or fretted, even harmonics.

- ✔ **In the second measure, you don't cut off the string in the bottom position; instead, you let the string sustain as you release pressure on the bar and return the note to its original pitch.**

- ✔ **Measure three is just like measure two except before you change directions and begin the return, you graze the string at the 12th fret, sounding a harmonic.**
  So that's down on an open string, up on a harmonic. You only strike the string once.

- ✔ **Measure four is just like measure three except you hammer a finger into the fifth fret and return on a new note, A.**

Figure 12-3:
Playing
trem-bar
dives.

© John Wiley & Sons, Inc.

These techniques can be played on any note, whether the note is an open string or a fretted note. Try playing through Figure 12-3, applying each variation to the fifth string, fourth string, and so on. Try fretting a note and playing dives and dive returns. From a fretted note, you can hammer on to another note with another finger before a return.

In Figure 12-4, you work with the same dive-and-return techniques from the last example, but using harmonics. You focus on the natural harmonic at the fifth fret of the third string. In order to get maximum sustain and volume out of harmonics like this, you need to play loud and with a lot of distortion, so be sure to turn up your amp's drive and overall level.

You dive approximately a fifth down, but again it's not necessary to focus on that degree of change specifically with these examples. In fact, you can experiment with how far you dive and even how far you return. My examples return to the original pitches, but you can pull up on the bar to return the pitch to a note higher than the original, depending on your tremolo system's range of movement. In measure three, you first strike the string open and then graze a harmonic before diving. In measure four, you dive the open string and return with a harmonic.

Figure 12-4:
Playing
harmonic
trem-bar
dives.

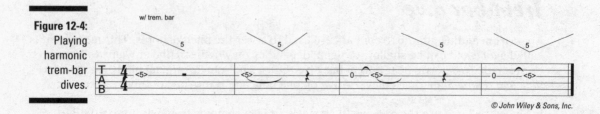

© John Wiley & Sons, Inc.

When diving and returning, some players initially set a string into motion by flicking it with a finger on their fretting hands instead of picking it in a normal fashion. This leaves the picking hand free to operate the bar. You can also swing the trem bar around so that it points away from the strings and then pull *up* on it to dive down. Pantera guitarist Dimebag Darrell used these techniques along with gobs of distortion and loads of level to perform his trademark harmonic squeals, which were simply open-string dives and harmonic returns.

There are many ways in which guitarists dive and return notes and harmonics using a trem bar. You can pick up on ideas by listening to others. A few good places to start are Stevie Ray Vaughan's "Little Wing," Van Halen's "Eruption," and Jimi Hendrix's "The Star-Spangled Banner." For more subtle usage, listen to Chris Isaak's "Wicked Game" and Heart's "Barracuda." Alex Lifeson's guitar solo in Rush's "Limelight" is an excellent example of how to use trem-bar vibrato, dives, and returns using open strings, harmonics, and fretted notes.

Figure 12-5 is an example of diving and returning on a chord. When the A-minor chord is raked backward using a clean tone with reverb, the dive and return is very reminiscent of surf music from the 1960s — specifically, "Bombora" by The Surfaris and songs from The Ventures and The Shadows. Though not considered surf music, "Hanky Panky" by Tommy James and the Shondells is another good example of diving and retuning on a chord.

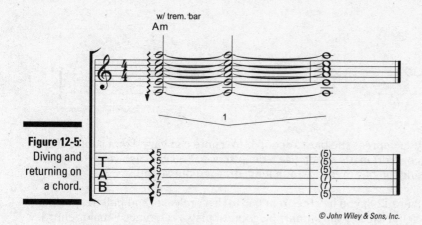

© John Wiley & Sons, Inc.

Figure 12-5:
Diving and
returning on
a chord.

Trem-bar dip

When guitarists perform a very quick and short dive and release, and do so immediately upon striking a note, it's called a *dip*. In Figure 12-6, you play an E triad in the 12th position, dipping into each note. In the notation, the narrow downward/upward line instructs you to dip. The number in the middle of the line indicates how far you should dip — in this case, one step. In this example, it's not critical that you dip precisely one whole step, only that you dip enough to dive and lower the pitch a bit. This embellishment can be used to decorate or ornament notes as you play through scales, melodies, riffs, and solos.

Figure 12-6:
Playing
trem-bar
dips.

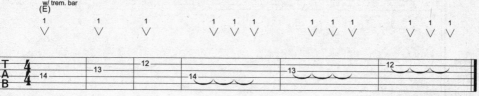

© John Wiley & Sons, Inc.

Trem-bar scoop

When guitarists depress the bar *before* striking a note, and then release the pressure on the bar so that the pitch quickly rises to the target note, it's called a *scoop*. Scoops create the impression that you're bending or sliding into a note, but with a unique sound quality that comes only from a trem bar. Like dips, scoops are used to embellish notes in your lead lines, like Steve Vai does in his rendition of "Christmas Time Is Here" beginning at 0:51. You can also scoop into chords, like Vernon Reid does using an open-position D chord at the 0:17 mark of Living Colour's "Broken Hearts."

In Figure 12-7, you play an E5 power chord in the seventh position, scooping into each note. Different notation programs use different markings to represent this technique. Above the tab in my example, you first see a number, indicating how far to depress the bar, followed by a dotted line that instructs you to depress the bar before striking the string, finishing with an upward-pointing line representing the rise in pitch to the target note. You need to cut off each note before starting a new scoop; otherwise, you'll produce a dive. I give the last note some trem-arm vibrato as I let it sustain.

Figure 12-7:
Playing
trem-bar
scoops.

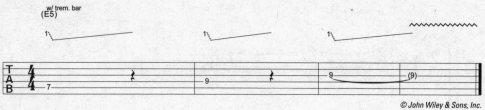

© John Wiley & Sons, Inc.

The degree to which you depress the bar to scoop into a note can vary. For a subtle effect, use a shallow scoop. For a dramatic effect, use a deep scoop. You can also vary the quickness, by slowly releasing the bar pressure for a long, dragged-out scoop.

In the last example, Figure 12-8, you use the trem bar to dive, release, and pull to specific pitches. The figure is set in the key of F. It may be good to play a reference F-major chord in order to get your ear oriented to this key. The melody is fretted and played normally in the first two measures so that you can hear what pitches to target with the trem bar in the measures that follow. After you get the melody in your head, start at measure three, which begins with a natural harmonic at the 12th fret of the third string. This note is the second of the F-major scale, G. From this G note, you move backward and forward in the F scale, reproducing the same melody from the previous measures and changing pitches by using the trem bar only as the string sustains. Because you get to one note in the line, A, by pulling up on the trem bar, this example requires a floating system with that kind of range.

Figure 12-8:
Changing
notes with a
trem bar.

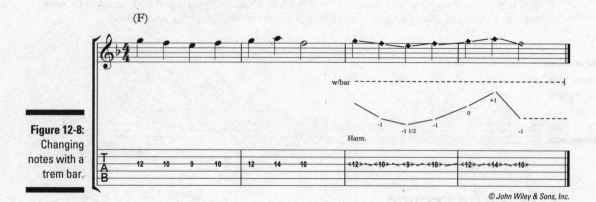

© John Wiley & Sons, Inc.

Looking at measures three and four in Figure 12-8, you see one harmonic at the 12th fret of the third string that sustains through to the end of the example. Above the tab, you see lines representing the movement of your trem bar and numbers indicating how far away to go from the original pitch in steps. Unlike the rest of the examples in this chapter, here it's critical to dive and pull to specific pitches. For this reason, it's a good idea to know the melody first.

The first time you try to play Figure 12-8, you'll likely miss the proper pitches. Instead of shooting for the whole thing right out of the gate, first focus on the first pitch change from G to F, which is a whole step down. Fret and play the two notes in a normal manner, as you do in measure one; then match those same pitches with the harmonic and trem-bar dive. In time, you get a feel for how much pressure to apply to the trem bar in order to go down a perfect whole step to F from G. Rehearse this move until you do it well with consistency. Then work on adding the next note following the same process.

In all, this is how the whole phrase is played:

1. **Strike a G harmonic at the 12th fret of the third string and sustain it throughout the entire melodic phrase.**

2. **Push the bar down enough to sound an F, which is a whole step below G.**

3. **From F, push the bar down just a little more to sound the note a half step lower, E.**

4. **From E, release enough pressure to bring the string tension back to F.**

5. **From F, release the bar pressure completely, returning to the original pitch, G.**

6. **From G, pull up on the bar to increase the string tension by a whole step and produce the pitch, A.**

7. **From A, release the pull and begin to push until you pass G and hit the tonic, F.**

Using an electronic tuner with automatic note detection is a good way to double-check that these dives are in tune.

Playing melodies like this isn't easy. It requires a good ear, a lot of control, and a lot of practice, but the end result is very cool. For a great example of this technique, listen to Jeff Beck's beautiful rendition of "Somewhere over the Rainbow." Many live versions are available on YouTube with great close-ups of Jeff's right hand and trem-bar usage. Notice how he forgoes the pick and plucks the strings with his thumb while his fingers rest on the trem bar. Look even closer and you'll see that he performs volume swells with his little finger on the volume knob. Pretty slick!

Part V
Practice Makes Perfect

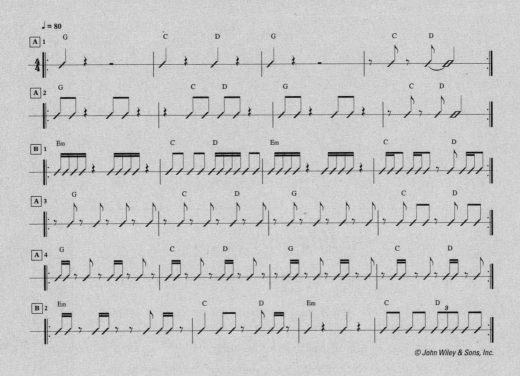

Practice guitar using accompaniments and tracks in an article at
www.dummies.com/extras/guitarrhythmandtechnique.

In this part . . .

- ✔ Review quarter, eighth, and sixteenth notes to sharpen your rhythm playing.

- ✔ Work with tempos, measures, beats, and rests to improve your timing.

- ✔ Prepare to read music and follow charts.

- ✔ Play melodic patterns to hone your chops and add interest to your lead lines.

- ✔ Get your fingers in shape and ready for the big leagues.

Chapter 13

Running Down Your Rhythms

In This Chapter

▶ Working with rhythm exercises

▶ Preparing to read music and follow charts

▶ Access the audio tracks and video clips at www.dummies.com/go/guitarrhythmtechnique

*I*n this chapter, you work with exercises designed to help you run down the rhythms from Parts I and II. Use these drills to improve your reading and playing of rhythms. As tedious as these examples may be to master, they get easier the more you do them, and they prepare you to break down and play rhythms encountered in songs as you venture out into the world of music.

Slow and Simple

Figure 13-1 falls into the category of slow and simple, but that doesn't mean that it's going to be easy. If counting and playing rhythms is still new to you, the exercise will be a challenge. Be patient as you work out the rhythms, and keep in mind that the end goal here is not to memorize the figure, but to play it while you read it.

As you work through this figure in the key of G, I recommend that you follow these steps:

1. **Give a listen to Audio Track 45, just to familiarize yourself with it.**

2. **Work out each measure one by one, rehearsing at your own pace and repeating parts as you work toward completing a section.**

3. **When you get a section (one line) down, try reading and playing it along with the audio track before moving on.**

   Your end goal is to play the figure beginning to end, first on your own and at your own pace, and then with the recording, referring to the slash notation as you go.

As you follow these steps, keep in mind the following tips:

✔ As you follow the chord changes, play full chords, power chords, or single notes in any position or register you like, using either an acoustic or electric guitar, and not worrying about copying my type of sound on the audio track.

✔ As long as you play the rhythms as notated, it doesn't matter how you pick and strum them. Use whichever combination of downstrokes and upstrokes feels best to you.

✔ Count out the rhythms before you play them, even penciling them in below the slash notation if doing so helps. Using 1, 2, 3, 4, for quarter notes; 1 and 2 and 3 and 4 and, for eighth notes; 1 e and a, 2 e and a, 3 e and a, 4 e and a, for sixteenth notes (or 1 e & a, and so on); and 1 trip-let, 2 trip-let, 3 trip-let, 4 trip-let, for triplets. For example, the first measure in the last line (section B2) is counted: 1 e (and), 2 e (and), (3) and, 4 e (and). As you write, you can either put rests in parentheses or not write anything in for them at all.

Figure 13-1:
Slow and
simple.

Notice that you have eighth and sixteenth notes joined together by beams. The last measure in section B is counted "1 e and," with the eighth note on the end getting both the "and" and the "a" of a sixteenth-note set.

Use left- and right-hand damping and muting to properly play rests.

Moderate and Meaty

Next, in Figure 13-2, you step things up a bit with a faster tempo and more rhythms in the mix. For reference, listen to Audio Track 46. As you play through these exercises in the key of A, follow the same steps and suggestions from the preceding section by working things out one measure at a time and rehearsing parts individually before attempting to make a pass through the whole thing.

You can play the chords in any fashion you want, even using single notes. What you play with downstrokes and upstrokes is your choice, too.

Figure 13-2: Moderate and meaty.

© John Wiley & Sons, Inc.

Notice that you have eighth and sixteenth notes joined together by beams. The first measure in section A3 is counted "1 and a," with the first eighth note getting both the 1 and the "e" of a sixteenth-note set.

TIP

The first measure in section A4 is counted "1 a." Imagine it as a full set of sixteenth notes. The first three parts of the beats, "1 e and," are equal to a dotted eighth note; then you have one sixteenth note left at the end of the beam. So, you strike the strings on "1" and then on "a." This rhythm is flipped in the first measure of section B2 with the sixteenth note at the beginning of the set. In this case, you play on "1" and "e" and you sustain "e" through to the end of the sixteenth-note set.

Fast and Furious

Figure 13-3 is the most challenging of the three exercises in this chapter. Not only has the tempo increased again, but the rhythms have become more difficult, too. As you play through these exercises in the key of A minor, follow the same steps as before, familiarizing yourself with each section measure by measure before making a pass through the whole thing. At the end of the third line, section B1, I break away from chords and play single notes that outline an E-major triad. You can stick with strumming the chord or follow me on the triad.

PLAY THIS!

Familiarize yourself with the figure by listening to Audio Track 47; then play along with it when you're ready.

Figure 13-3:
Fast and
furious.

TIP

Reading a score

Guitar players are notoriously bad sight-readers and often completely overlook notation in favor of tab. I don't consider this to be such a bad thing. After all, it's what the finished product sounds like that matters, not whether you read a piece of sheet music to get there.

That said, there's no reason to ignore information that's very useful and helps to expedite the learning process. Even if you can't read everything in a score, you can still peek at the notation to pick up on the rhythms. As you learn songs from transcribed scores that feature tab and notation, make it a point to follow the rhythms while listening to the recorded song, stopping the recording to count and work out the rhythms on the page. The more you do this, the better you'll be able to read rhythms on the fly and pick up on new parts quickly.

If you have aspirations of playing professionally, you'll be expected, at the very least, to read basic charts with rhythmic slash notation and be able to talk with others about tempos, measures, beats, and rests.

Chapter 14

Picking through Scales with Melodic Patterns

• •

In This Chapter

▶ Using melodic patterns

▶ Improving dexterity and synchronization

▶ Access the audio tracks and video clips at www.dummies.com/go/guitarrhythmtechnique

• •

You don't always see guitarists playing straight up and down scale patterns. Riffs and melodies move through scales in various ways, often skipping notes and repeating others. Additionally, lead lines make use of a composition technique called *melodic patterns,* which is a method of ascending and descending scales by repeating some type of note sequence on each scale degree as you go. Sometimes referred to as *scale sequences* or *picking patterns* by guitarists, melodic patterns work well as exercises to improve your dexterity, are especially useful for synchronizing your picking and fretting hands, and can even be used to practice hammer-ons and pull-offs.

By the Numbers

Before you get going with melodic patterns, you need to understand how numbers are used when teaching the technique. When writing out scales, numbers normally refer to interval structure. For example, see the following sample scales:

Major scale: 1–2–3–4–5–6–7

Minor scale: 1–2–♭3–4–5–♭6–♭7

Major pentatonic: 1–2–3–5–6

Minor pentatonic: 1–♭3–4–5–♭7

When teaching melodic patterns, however, numbers are used sequentially to physically count the notes in a given pattern without regard to intervals. This is true no matter what type of scale pattern you play. You think: The first note in the pattern, the second note in the pattern, the third note in the pattern, and so on. You don't start over after reaching the octave either. You keep counting in sequential order. Keep this in mind as you work through this chapter.

Melodic Patterns in Groups of Three

The typical way to get started with melodic patterns is to ascend and descend a scale pattern in staggered groups of three or four. In this section, you get started with groups of three in the pentatonic scale. Here's how it works:

Imagine the scale as a series of numbers that does not restart register to register. For example, 1–2–3–4–5–6–7–8–9–10, and so on. Start on the first scale degree and play up three notes; then play up three notes from the second scale degree; then do the same thing from the third scale degree; and so on. When written out in numbers, the melodic pattern looks like this:

1–2–3, 2–3–4, 3–4–5, 4–5–6, and so on

Now that you have the idea of how this melodic pattern works, listen to Audio Track 48 to hear how it sounds, and look at Figure 14-1 to see it tabbed out using A-minor pentatonic scale pattern 1. In the tab, you see precisely where to place your fingers on the fretboard in order to progress through the scale using the three-note sequence.

Figure 14-1: Melodic pattern in groups of three using the pentatonic scale.

© John Wiley & Sons, Inc.

As you begin to put this melodic pattern to use, it works best to first focus on ascending, as you see in measures one through three of Figure 14-1. Additionally, I recommend that you work on joining two groups of three together as I instruct you to do in the following list. As you work through Figure 14-1, follow these steps:

1. **Work out the first three notes of the figure at your own pace, and be sure to alternate your pick beginning with the downstroke.**

2. **Add the next set of three notes, which ought to begin with an upstroke on C at the eighth fret of the sixth string.**

3. **Back up and play through the first two groups of three notes, joining them together using strict alternate picking with no breaks.**

   Rehearse this much until you can play it fluidly and without thinking.

4. **Move to strings five and four (the second half of measure one) and work out and rehearse the next two groups of three notes.**

5. **Continue with playing two groups of three notes by starting on the fourth, third, and second strings, being sure to follow the layout of the pentatonic notes.**

6. **Ascend the pentatonic scale pattern by joining together all groups of notes using strict alternate picking with no breaks as you move note group to note group.**

In Chapter 10, you're taught to plant your picking hand on the guitar in order to have the most control of the pick while you alternate it. I recommend you do that in this chapter. Also, don't use a flimsy pick for exercises like Figure 14-1. Instead, work with a pick in the medium to heavy range.

When you get used to ascending the pentatonic scale in groups of three, you can resume Figure 14-1 by beginning at measure four, where you descend the scale with the same melodic pattern. In this case, everything has been reversed. Think of the highest-pitched note in the pattern, the C at the eighth fret of the first string, as one, and then number the notes sequentially from there as you move down the pattern. It works well to join and rehearse two groups of three in this direction as well. Even though everything has been reversed, I recommend you still start with a downstroke, for now.

You may find ascending the pentatonic easier than descending, because you use the more efficient inside picking on your way up. If you begin your descent with an upstroke, however, you can take advantage of inside picking on your way down, too.

A good goal to work toward is playing Figure 14-1 at the rate of 80 BPM. From there, you can set your metronome tempo higher and higher, gradually increasing your speed over time, but always being sure to finger the notes cleanly and pick the strings accurately.

You can hear examples of this group-of-three melodic pattern in Led Zeppelin's "Good Times Bad Times" beginning at 2:03 using the E-minor pentatonic, and ZZ Top's "La Grange" beginning at 1:11 in C-minor pentatonic. For more examples, listen to Ace Frehley's "Ozone," beginning at 2:13 in D-major/B-minor pentatonic, and Los Lonely Boys' "Heaven," beginning at 2:13 in G-major pentatonic (with an added fourth), both of which feature guitars tuned down one half-step to E♭.

The A-minor pentatonic scale in Figure 14-1 can also be used in its relative C-major tonality by simply starting on C rather than A. In other words, begin halfway through the first measure. When you get comfortable playing in a scale pattern, you should work out the same note sequence in other scale patterns in the same key. For example, play using groups of three notes in all five A-minor/C-major pentatonic scale patterns. When you're finished, practice doing the same thing in other pentatonic keys.

Spend a few minutes or more each day practicing melodic patterns in order to develop dexterity, synchronize your hands, and get to know scale patterns better.

As you know from Chapter 7, guitarists don't always pick every note they play. Instead, they often use articulations to sound notes. This remains true while using melodic patterns. Figure 14-2 is a repeat of Figure 14-1, but with the addition of hammer-ons and pull-offs. In order to save space, I don't notate the entire scale pattern beginning to end. Instead, I give you just enough to get going in both directions. You take it from there.

As you play through Figure 14-2, your goal should be to sound each note with an equal amount of force whether you pick, hammer on, or pull off, so be sure to execute the articulations cleanly. With the added hammer-ons and pull-offs, this melodic pattern becomes an even better exercise in increasing your fretting-hand dexterity and strength. Furthermore, the use of articulations produces a flowing, legato sound. Be sure to use these hammer-ons and pull-offs in other pentatonic patterns and keys.

Figure 14-2:
Melodic
pattern in
groups of
three using
hammer-ons
and pull-offs
with the
pentatonic
scale.

© John Wiley & Sons, Inc.

In situations where hammer-ons and pull-offs are in use, many guitarists *phantom pick* — that is, they maintain the downstroke and upstroke movement so that picked notes are struck with the same strokes used when alternate picking is in use. (See the pick-stroke symbols in Figure 14-2.) This method of picking helps you stay in step with the pulse and rhythm.

Technically, you can add additional hammer-ons and pull-offs to Figure 14-2. In the first measure, when you finish the second group of three notes, you can pull off to the fifth fret of the fifth string instead of picking it. This remains true as you work your way up the scale pattern. Coming down, you can add a hammer-on after the second group of three notes. Whether to pick the beginning of each new group as I notate or add hammer-ons and pull-offs is your call. Obviously, the more you hammer on and pull off, the less you pick and the more legato your playing sounds.

As you work through the melodic patterns presented in this chapter, take time to get comfortable with each one before moving onto the next. You may take a few minutes, a few hours, or a few days with each one. There's no rush here.

Next, in Figure 14-3, you use the three-note melodic pattern from the previous examples again, but this time in a major scale. You can play melodic patterns in any variety of major scale pattern, but I chose one that features three notes per string because I feel it works out a little better fingering-wise. Specifically, you use a C-major scale pattern beginning at the eighth fret of the sixth string. You can hear what Figure 14-3 sounds like in Audio Track 49.

Because major scales have more notes and more complex scale patterns, applying a melodic pattern is more challenging here than it is with pentatonic scales. With extra patience and practice, though, your fingers will catch on. As with the previous figures, take things one half-measure at a time, rehearsing small portions of the scale as you slowly work toward adding more. When you're able to smoothly ascend the scale, change directions.

If completing a whole position is proving to be too much for you, try playing through only one octave of the scale.

When you get used to playing Figure 14-3, work your way through other major-scale patterns and keys using the same melodic pattern. As you do, you may find that some patterns and positions are more easily fingered than others. It's okay to play to your strengths by favoring the areas that work best for you.

In addition to picking each and every note as you work your way through a major scale using a three-note melodic pattern, you can use hammer-ons and pull-offs as shown in Figure 14-4. I partially get you started in both directions, leaving the rest to you to finish.

Figure 14-3:
Melodic pattern in groups of three using the major scale.

© John Wiley & Sons, Inc.

Figure 14-4:
Melodic pattern in groups of three using hammer-ons and pull-offs with the major scale.

© John Wiley & Sons, Inc.

Because major scales have more notes and more complex patterns than pentatonic scales, the amount of hammering on and pulling off is greatly increased from the previous pentatonic examples. In Figure 14-4, each new group of three notes in the melodic pattern begins with a pickstroke, which is how I recommend you first play the figure. Another option is to play in a legato style by picking only on string changes. For instance, in Figure 14-4 the eighth-note triplet at the end of beat one would slur right into beat two. If you go this route, you run into long chains of hammer-ons and pull-offs, which require a lot of dexterity and strength to maintain. Playing in a legato manner like this is a trademark technique of Joe Satriani. For an example, listen to his song "Always with Me, Always with You" beginning at 2:58. In case you're wondering, Joe doesn't employ phantom picking during his long legato lines.

Sometimes a slide works better than a pull-off or hammer-on. As I descend in Figure 14-4, I like to transition from the tenth to the ninth fret of the third string by sliding my first finger down (hence, the legato slide marking in the tab).

Melodic Patterns in Groups of Four

Another common grouping of notes that is used when playing melodic patterns is groups of four. With this pattern, you start on a scale degree and play up four steps, and then move to the next scale degree and play up four steps, and so on. When written out, it looks like this:

1–2–3–4, 2–3–4–5, 3–4–5–6, 4–5–6–7, and so on

You play in groups of four using the A-minor pentatonic scale pattern 1 in Figure 14-5. You ascend on the first line and descend on the second line. Listen to Audio Track 50 to hear what the melodic pattern sounds like. I recommend that you work out and rehearse this new pattern in two groups of four, which is a half-measure at a time. Be sure to maintain steady alternate picking, first by beginning with a downstroke in both directions, and then, for variation and an extra challenge, by starting each way with an upstroke. Play at your own pace and set a goal to reach 80 BPM. Over time, you can work toward playing at higher tempos, using other pentatonic-scale patterns, and transposing to new keys.

Figure 14-5: Melodic pattern in groups of four using the pentatonic scale.

When playing in groups of four using pentatonic-scale patterns, you often end a group with the same finger that starts the next group. In this situation, your options are either to reuse the same finger by barring a pair of strings with it, or to use another finger, perhaps one that you may not normally use when playing the pentatonic straight up.

There aren't any correct fingerings to use at all times; you go with what best enables you to get the job done.

Figure 14-6 is a repeat of Figure 14-5, but this time using hammer-ons and pull-offs. The tab gets you partially started in each direction. You can complete the rest on your own. Also, I have you pick the first note of each four-note group, but you could go full legato and pick only on string changes.

Figure 14-6:
Melodic pattern in groups of four using hammer-ons and pull-offs with the pentatonic scale.

© John Wiley & Sons, Inc.

Next, in Figure 14-7, you play in groups of four using the same C-major scale pattern as Figures 14-3 and 14-4. Listen to Audio Track 51 to hear what the melodic pattern sounds like.

With major scales, it doesn't help to work out the groups of notes two at a time. Instead, I recommend that you visually keep track of each scale degree as you use it to start a four-note group, and look ahead to the next starting point as you go. It's also helpful to work with only a section of the major-scale pattern at a time rather than try to go the whole distance right out of the gate. You can gradually add more groups of notes as you become more comfortable with the fingerings, picking, and melodic pattern. Be sure to maintain steady alternate picking, first by beginning with a downstroke in both directions, and then, for variation and an extra challenge, by starting each way with an upstroke. Play at your own pace and set a goal to reach 80 BPM. Over time, you can work toward playing at higher tempos, using other major-scale patterns, and transposing to new keys.

The next step is to repeat the melodic pattern from the previous example, but do so using hammer-ons and pull-offs, as shown in Figure 14-8. I chose to always pick the first note of each four-note group, but you're free to experiment with playing more legato by picking only on string changes. The tab gets you started on playing in both directions. You take it from there. This example can be played at higher tempos, using other major-scale patterns, and transposing to new keys as well.

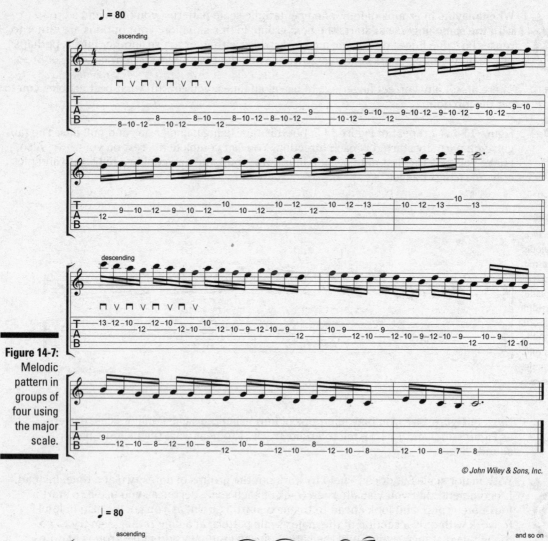

Figure 14-7:
Melodic pattern in groups of four using the major scale.

© John Wiley & Sons, Inc.

Figure 14-8:
Melodic pattern in groups of four using hammer-ons and pull-offs with the major scale.

© John Wiley & Sons, Inc.

Melodic Patterns in Thirds

Another popular melodic pattern is one where you play in groups of two, but each group uses scale tones that are a third apart. You could consider this a leap-frogging melodic pattern, because thirds are based on the playing of every other note. It looks like this:

1–3, 2–4, 3–5, 4–6, and so on

This is best understood and played using the major scale, so that's where you start in Figure 14-9, using the same C-major scale patterns as earlier. By now, you know the drill. As you play in thirds, work out the major-scale pattern in sections, slowly working toward completing the whole thing. Listen to Audio Track 52 for reference. When you're ready, play through other types of major-scale patterns, using different positions, and transposing to new keys.

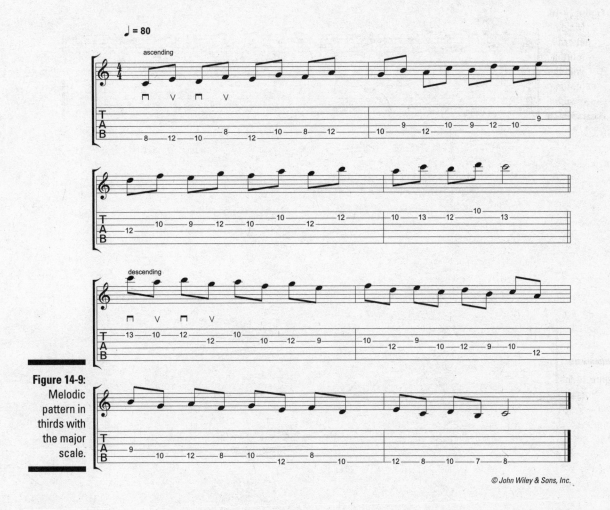

Figure 14-9: Melodic pattern in thirds with the major scale.

You can apply a concept similar to Figure 14-9 (Audio Track 53) to the pentatonic scale. Instead of being true thirds, Figure 14-10 is really just leapfrogging the tones in the A minor pentatonic scale 1–3, 2–4, 3–5, 4–6, and so on. When the pentatonic scale is played in this manner, the actual interval between scale degrees one and three is a fourth. In fact, all the intervals are fourths except the interval between the second and fourth notes in the pattern, which is a major third. Because most of the interval jumps are fourths, many guitarists call this a melodic pattern in fourths. You can use this movement in other pentatonic-scale patterns, in different positions, and transposing to new keys. You hear the same concept used in the key of F throughout Fleetwood Mac's "As Long As You Follow."

Figure 14-10:
Melodic pattern in "fourths" with the pentatonic scale.

Part VI
The Part of Tens

Find ten steps to singing and playing guitar at the same time in an article at
www.dummies.com/extras/guitarrhythmtechnique.

In this part . . .

✔ Look at ten tracks loaded with valuable guitar techniques for you to play and practice.

✔ Get to know ten titans of technique whom you can turn to for inspiration.

Chapter 15

Ten Technique Tracks

▶ Honing your chops with ten well-known songs
▶ Working on your right-hand and left-hand skills

In this chapter, I introduce you to ten songs that are not only well known but also well suited for adding an array of guitar techniques to your playing. The list runs the gamut from acoustic to electric, from soft rock to heavy metal. I offer examples that are useful to both rhythm and lead guitarists and that give you the chance to work on both your right- and left-hand skills.

"Purple Haze" (1967)

This is probably the best-known Jimi Hendrix song. Although much has been said about the guitar solo, it's the opening guitar riffing that puts it on my list. After a few measures of tri-tones, the main and most recognizable riff begins by sliding, bending, and hammering its way through E-minor pentatonic scale patterns, in a manner not too far off from another Hendrix song, "Voodoo Child (Slight Return)." The verses to "Purple Haze" feature the changes E7#9-G-A, with the G and A played in Hendrix's signature style of wrapping the thumb around the neck to fret roots on the sixth string.

I should also mention Hendrix's guitar solos to "Hey Joe" and "The Wind Cries Mary." They're loaded with what has become standard lead-guitar licks and phrases.

"Stairway to Heaven" (1971)

This Led Zeppelin classic is a cornucopia of guitar styles and techniques. Guitarist Jimmy Page made use of acoustic guitars, electric guitars, and even 12-string guitars in the studio. There are soft moments, like the song's delicately fingerpicked introduction, and moments of high intensity, like the guitar solo and final verses. It runs the dynamics gamut in a way few songs do. This is also one of the few songs that I recommend for guitar players to learn all parts. From fingerpicking, to sixteenth-note strum patterns, to chord arpeggiation, from hammer-ons, to pull-offs, to slides, to bends, from alternate picking, to dampening and scratching, "Stairway," like heaven itself, has it all.

"Free Bird" (1974)

This national treasure from southern rock band Lynyrd Skynyrd clocks in at over nine minutes long, with more than half of it an extended guitar solo. Need I say more? It starts out as a power ballad, with Gary Rossington adding the song's main melodic hook on slide guitar. At 4:42, the tempo picks up and lead guitarist Allen Collins takes over. What follows may very well be the longest recorded guitar solo to ever become a classic rock radio staple, one that triggers an air guitar frenzy whenever it's heard. The number of bends is enough to shred anything but the most well-callused fingers, and the rate at which you must repeat pull-offs is fast enough to spark a fire.

More than anything, the solo is a master class in motifs, because each section is highlighted by short, repeated melodic ideas. You want to get this one under your belt if only to honor the next barroom request for "FREE BIRD!" It's one of the best closers in the business.

"Wish You Were Here" (1975)

You can easily get a crowded barroom to sing along with this classic Pink Floyd song, but it makes the list because of the acoustic guitar solo that begins at 0:58. Though properly playing all the bends using an acoustic guitar with typical, heavy-gauge strings like you hear in the recording is difficult, it becomes fairly easy to play when you use an electric guitar, or an acoustic guitar with extra-light strings that don't have a wound G. In fact, when played with light, electric-gauge strings, it becomes one of the best ways to ease your way into lead-guitar playing because of its simple use of hammer-ons, pull-offs, slides, and bends, plus its slow tempo and the amount of space between phrases. The song is set in the key of E minor/G major, but the very same techniques and phrases can be transposed to other positions and keys to play lead-guitar lines on other songs and in other styles of music. Along with this song, any David Gilmour guitar solo can teach you a lot about bending and phrasing.

"Hotel California" (1977)

Three words: extended guitar solo! There are so many elements to this song by the Eagles that make it one of the most popular rock songs ever recorded, but be honest: It's the tasty licks by lead guitarists Don Felder and Joe Walsh that give you goose bumps and leave you hanging on every note. Both men are masters of phrasing and put on a clinic as they navigate the chord changes with bends, slides, hammer-ons, and pull-offs. Felder starts out the solo section that begins at 4:20 and then hands it over to Walsh at 4:46. After each one has made a pass through the whole progression, they trade licks back and forth before coming together to create the most memorable harmonized guitar line in all of rock 'n' roll. This final part consists of two guitars a third apart using pull-offs to play triads that outline each chord in the progression. The acoustic, 12-string opening is worth a play through, too, because it serves as a good example of using a capo and arpeggiation, with a few unique chord shapes and distinct embellishments thrown in.

"Dust in the Wind" (1978)

The original single of this song by Kansas sold a million copies on vinyl when it was first released, and then went gold again as a digital download 25 years later, which is a real testament to its influence and staying power. It remains a guitar staple, too, with its fingerpicking pattern being one of the most common and useful to know. Similar finger patterns are used in "Blackbird" by The Beatles and "Landslide" by Fleetwood Mac.

"Pride and Joy" (1983)

This is one of the best-known songs from the legendary Texas bluesman, Stevie Ray Vaughan. It's a shuffle set to a standard 12-bar blues chord progression in E, with guitars tuned down a half-step to E♭. Although this song features great guitar solos that are worth taking a look at, my focus here is the main guitar figure based on a boogie-woogie-style walking bass line. It has two main elements that make it unique:

- ✔ **Instead of cleanly picking each note in the bass line, Vaughan strikes multiple strings with each downstroke, being sure to mute everything but his target note.** The result is that all notes on the beat have a raking quality to them, which thickens up the sound and produces a percussive-like effect.

- ✔ **Vaughan lifts his hand on all upbeats and strikes the first few open strings with upstrokes, emphasizing the short/long feel of the shuffle and further adding percussive impact.** This is a trademark SRV technique, which can also be heard in another well-known song of his, "Cold Shot."

"Master of Puppets" (1986)

Considered to be one of the best thrash metal songs ever, this Metallica concert staple from the band's early days in 1986 is loaded with heavily distorted and palm-muted riffery, the kind suitable for head banging and whipping around your long locks. At over eight and a half minutes long, the composition also includes pace-changing interludes featuring clean electric guitars and harmonized, melodic lines. True to the song's dynamic structure, the intermission doesn't stay subdued for too long before breaking into a full shred-fest led by lead guitarist Kirk Hammett. You won't get through the song without breaking a sweat, and you won't develop the necessary chops before breaking your hands with a lot of practice.

"Sweet Child o' Mine" (1988)

If Guns N' Roses guitarist, Slash, had not recorded anything other than this epic rock anthem, he would still be a legend. With guitars tuned down a half-step to E♭, the opening guitar riff is a good exercise in string skipping. The two solo sections between the verses are great examples of using pull-offs, hammer-ons, slides, and bends in a major key to play simple, lyrical lead lines. The song gets more exciting at 3:35 as the music changes keys and Slash weaves his way melodically through the E harmonic minor scale in haunting fashion. Finally, at 4:03, the volcano erupts, and Slash unleashes one of the most devastating and face-melting solos ever put to tape. It's a master class in high-intensity, in-your-face lead licks and full of chops galore.

"Tears in Heaven" (1992)

A guitar song can't get more soft and tender than this nylon-string masterpiece from Eric Clapton. Even though it was recorded using a classical guitar, it can still be played on a regular steel-stringed acoustic or electric. The whole piece is played without a pick and features a finger pattern that is fairly simple and intuitive, with moments where you claw at a chord piano-style, and moments where you alternate your thumb and fingers. Instead of using typical chord shapes, you play unique voicings that include inversions, partial chord forms, and alternate bass notes. On top of all this is the two-guitar interplay with hooky hammer-on, pull-off, and slide fills.

Chapter 16

Ten (Or So) Guitarists to Inspire Your Rhythm and Technique

● ●

In This Chapter

▶ Finding inspiration among the greats

▶ Looking at guitarists with skills worth developing

● ●

Rhythms and techniques don't have much appeal or meaning in and of themselves. It's when you hear guitarists use rhythms and techniques in musical and expressive ways that your interest is piqued and you get inspired. This is why I feature so many references to popular songs and famous guitar players throughout this book — to connect the technical information to something familiar and direct you to where each concept can be further explored and developed.

In this chapter, I remind you of guitar players who have styles you can work with to increase your skills and develop your sense of rhythm.

This is not a list of the greatest and best, nor is it comprehensive. The number of influential guitar players who have skills worthy of examination is great — too great to mention them all here. The number of techniques that are possible on the guitar, and the level to which you can take them, are beyond the scope of this chapter as well. My focus is simply to list some well-known guitarists with a large catalog of recognizable songs from which useful and inspiring concepts can be drawn and applied to your playing.

Chet Atkins C.G.P. (1924–2001)

This country gentleman is for serious fingerpickers only. Chet is one of the most respected musicians in the history of country music, and highly regarded among guitar players specifically for his complex, finger-style technique. Influenced early on by the alternating bass-note patterns of Merle Travis, Chet took to a thumbpick and fingers approach to playing that featured chords, melody, bass lines, and influences from classical, flamenco, folk, bluegrass, country, and blues styles. Some of his trademark instrumental songs include "Galloping on Guitar," "Windy and Warm," "Yakety Axe," "Country Gentleman," and "Mister Sandman."

By the way, *C.G.P.* stands for the lighthearted, Atkins-coined title "Certified Guitar Player," an honorary degree he bestowed not only on himself but also on other guitarists he felt contributed to the legacy of guitar playing such as Tommy Emmanuel.

B.B. King (1925–)

With one of the most recognizable styles in guitardom, B.B. King's string bending and vibrato has influenced nearly every blues guitarist who has followed him, along with many rock, jazz, and country players as well. Not known for using chords or playing rhythm guitar, King prefers to stick in tight positions (often referred to as "B.B.'s Box" in guitar circles) that feature a mixture of major and minor intervals, and chromatic steps. B.B. manages to squeeze a lot of licks out of only a handful of notes by varying his tone, attack, bending, vibrato, and phrasing.

One of his best-known songs is "The Thrill Is Gone," a purely minor-key number that is, ironically, not indicative of his signature guitar style. To hear his more trademark licks, listen to the 1965 album *Live at the Regal.* He also managed to lay down some of his classic lead lines in the song "When Loves Comes to Town," a surprisingly well-suited collaboration with U2.

Bob Dylan (1941–)

If you want to develop basic strumming skills with a little finger picking thrown in, look no further than Bob Dylan. From the simple strum patterns of "The Times They Are A-Changin'" and "Blowin' in the Wind" to fingerpicking selections like "Don't Think Twice, It's Alright" and "One Too Many Mornings," Dylan provides everything you need to sharpen your acoustic folk skills.

Jeff Beck (1944–)

Jeff Beck started out playing electric guitar in a conventional manner, but by the 1980s, he had completely abandoned the flatpick and made the use of his fingers and a tremolo system the defining characteristics of his sound and style. He likes to pluck the strings with his thumb while his fingers rest on the trem arm, which he keeps situated parallel to the strings. In this position, he can access the bar to perform dives, dips, and trills, all in midflight. Jeff was one of the first players to slide into a note by depressing the bar before striking the string (called a *scoop*), producing a sound effect that fools listeners into thinking he's using a metal or glass slide. One of the best examples of his whammy-bar work is "Where Were You" from the 1989 album *Jeff Beck's Guitar Shop.* The song is also featured on 2008's *Live at Ronnie Scott's.*

Tony Iommi (1948–)

Widely considered the godfather of heavy metal, Tony Iommi of Black Sabbath is a prolific pentatonic power-chord player considered by many to be the ultimate riff master. His solos are like a Lead Guitar 101 class, being primarily based in minor pentatonic patterns, featuring classic use of hammer-ons, pull-offs, slides, and bends, much in the same way as Kiss's Ace Frehley and AC/DC's Angus Young. For examples, listen to classic Black Sabbath songs like "Paranoid," "Iron Man," and "War Pigs," being sure to notice Tony's partiality for over-dubbing multiple guitar parts.

James Taylor (1948–)

You'll never see James Taylor strumming a guitar in the conventional manner. Instead, he uses strictly his thumb and fingers to pluck everything he plays. He doesn't play in a chord melody fashion like Martin Taylor (no relation) and Chet Atkins, but rather in a traditional folk finger-style manner that serves the purpose of supporting his vocals. For this reason, he's good listening for any singer/songwriter interested in taking a fingerpicking approach to guitar and accompaniment. One thing JT does well is chordal riffing, where standard open-position chords are embellished with added chord tones and extensions through the use of hammer-ons and pull-offs. He comes up with some unique chord shapes as well, usually ones that are the result of building voicings on alternate bass notes and pedal tones. He never travels without a capo, which allows him to make use of open strings and familiar chord shapes in various keys around the neck.

Check out JT's website (www.jamestaylor.com), where he has a series of free lessons that deconstruct some of his most beloved songs, including "Fire and Rain" and "Carolina in My Mind" through the use of revolutionary camera technology that allows you to see his right-hand technique from the inside of his guitar.

Mark Knopfler (1949–)

Lead guitarist, vocalist, and songwriter for the rock band Dire Straits, Mark Knopfler is a finger-style guitarist with a twist. He doesn't approach the guitar in a typical acoustic/fingerpicking/chord-melody manner; instead, he plays rock- and blues-flavored music on an electric guitar without using a pick. By plucking and popping the strings using primarily his index finger and thumb, Knopfler has a unique sound and feel that is best heard on his two biggest hits, "Sultans of Swing" and "Money for Nothing."

Bonnie Raitt (1949–)

Not too many ladies grow up with a passion for the music of old-school blues giants like Howlin' Wolf and Mississippi Fred McDowell, but Bonnie Raitt sure did. Raitt is an anomaly in that she excels at a technique and style dominated by male guitar players and put smoking slide guitar at the top of the mainstream radio charts. Raitt's open tunings and bottleneck fills are the sugarcoating to many of her hit songs, including "Something to Talk About," "Thing Called Love," and "Love Sneakin' Up on You."

Nile Rodgers (1952–)

Nile Rogers is not a household name, and unless you're up and up on the behind-the-scenes writers and producers who crafted some of the most memorable pop songs of the last 40 years, you probably haven't heard of him either. As a writer, producer, and guitarist, Rodgers has worked with Madonna, Duran Duran, David Bowie, The B52s, Diana Ross, Cyndi Lauper, Jeff Beck, Jimmie Vaughan, and Maroon 5, just to name a few. His catalog of work is also some of the most sampled music in the business and can be heard on many rap songs, including The Sugarhill Gang's "Rapper's Delight" and Will Smith's "Getting Jiggy Wit It."

Although Rodgers's talents and skills are many, he makes the list because he is an incredible rhythm guitar player who, along with James Brown guitarist Jimmy Nolan, pioneered and popularized what we now call *funk guitar*. If you want to learn how to make a song really groove with tight, syncopated, soulful, clean guitar rhythms and jazz-inflected chord voicings, look no further than classic disco songs like "Le Freak," "Good Times," "Dance, Dance, Dance," and "Everybody Dance," all by Rodgers's debut band, Chic. Also, try your hand at the guitar parts in Sister Sledge's "We Are Family," Diana Ross's "Upside Down," Madonna's "Like a Virgin," David Bowie's "Let's Dance," and Daft Punk's "Get Lucky."

Every single track that Niles Rodgers has recorded features his white 1959 Fender Stratocaster, known as "The Hitmaker." The total value of music to flow through the instrument was once valued at $2 billion, proving that Rodgers is a guitar force to be reckoned with. For a short lesson from the man himself, watch the YouTube video "Nile Rodgers Giggin Tips" at `http://youtu.be/CF-XDf_jf5w`.

Eddie Van Halen (1955–)

King Eddie is a very well-rounded musician who is equally skilled in lead guitar, rhythm guitar, harmony, and composition, but it's his tapping and whammy-bar techniques that made jaws drop and influenced the styles of so many guitarists that followed him like Randy Rhoads, Joe Satriani, and Steve Vai. Look no further than Van Halen's instrumental guitar solo, "Eruption," for a master class in dive bombs and tapped triads. He showcases his trademark tapping techniques on a nylon-string, acoustic guitar in "Spanish Fly." He was also highly skilled at playing harmonics, both pinch-harmonic squeaks like you hear in "Mean Street" and tapped harmonics like you hear in "Dance the Night Away."

Kirk Hammett (1962–)

Not only has Metallica sold a gazillion albums, but the band's lead guitarist, Kirk Hammett, has shredded a gazillion notes on most of those recordings. In fact, Hammett employs so much palm muting and fast, alternate picking that he tapes his picking hand in order to protect the skin from splitting and bleeding. If you're a fan of heavy music that features a lot of metal riffing and intricate solos, then Hammett's playing, particularly on Metallica's older albums like *Kill 'Em All, Ride the Lightning, Master of Puppets,* and *. . . And Justice for All,* is like Black Sabbath on steroids and features material suitable for any master class on shredding.

Appendix

Audio Tracks and Video Clips

∙∙∙

Sometimes, reading about a concept and trying to practice it just doesn't cut it — you need to see or hear it, too. Wherever you see the Play This icon, you find references to audio tracks and video clips that are available online. This appendix provides you with a handy list of all the audio tracks and video clips referenced throughout the book.

Discovering What's on the Audio Tracks

Table A-1 lists all the audio tracks that accompany each chapter.

Table A-1		Audio Tracks
Track Number	*Chapter*	*Description*
1	1	*Guitar Rhythm & Technique For Dummies* in a nutshell
2	2	Metronome example
3	2	Quarter notes and rests at 80 BPM
4	2	Quarter notes and rests at 90 BPM
5	2	Quarter notes and rests at 100 BPM
6	2	Half notes and rests at 100 BPM
7	2	Whole notes and rests at 100 BPM
8	2	Working with ties
9	2	Mix and mingle at 120 BPM
10	2	Waltz in 3/4 time
11	2	Dotted half notes
12	3	Exercising your eighths
13	4	Take the sixteenth notes and run
14	4	Sixteenth-note strum pattern 2
15	4	Sixteenth-note strum pattern 3
16	4	Sixteenth-note strum pattern 4
17	4	Sixteenth-note strum pattern 5
18	4	Sixteenth-note strum pattern 6
19	4	Sixteenth resting rhythm 1
20	4	Sixteenth resting rhythm 2
21	4	Sixteenth scratching 1
22	4	Sixteenth scratching 2

(Continued)

Table A-1 (*Continued*)

Track Number	Chapter	Description
23	4	Bo Diddley beat
24	4	Funky sixteenths, Step 1
25	4	Funky sixteenths, Step 2
26	4	Funky sixteenths, Step 3
27	4	Funky sixteenths, Step 4
28	4	Accenting sixteenths
29	5	Triplet example 1
30	5	Triplet example 2
31	5	Triplet rest
32	5	Tied triplets
33	5	Eighth-note shuffle 2
34	5	Eighth-note shuffle 3
35	5	Eighth-note shuffle 4
36	5	Triplet quarter note
37	5	12/8 example 1
38	5	12/8 example 2
39	5	12/8 example 3
40	9	Playing in drop-D tuning
41	9	Playing in double drop-D tuning
42	9	Playing in DADGAD tuning
43	9	Playing in open-E tuning
44	9	Playing in open-G tuning
45	13	Slow and simple
46	13	Moderate and meaty
47	13	Fast and furious
48	14	Melodic pattern in groups of three using the pentatonic scale
49	14	Melodic pattern in groups of three using the major scale
50	14	Melodic pattern in groups of four using the pentatonic scale
51	14	Melodic pattern in groups of four using the major scale
52	14	Melodic pattern in thirds with the major scale
53	14	Melodic pattern in "fourths" with the pentatonic scale

Looking at What's on the Video Clips

Table A-2 lists all the video clips that accompany each chapter.

Table A-2		Video Clips
Clip Number	**Chapter**	**Description**
1	1	*Guitar Rhythm & Technique For Dummies* in a nutshell
2	3	Strumming eighth notes
3	3	Playing eighth-note ties
4	3	Playing eighth-note rests
5	3	Strum pattern 1
6	3	Two chords per measure
7	3	Strum pattern 2: D D DUDU
8	3	Strum pattern 3: D DU UD
9	3	Working the upstrokes
10	3	Upstroke chord change 1
11	3	Upstroke chord change 2
12	3	Resting rhythm 1
13	3	Resting rhythm 2
14	3	Resting rhythm 3
15	3	Resting rhythm 4
16	3	String scratching 1
17	3	String scratching 2
18	3	String scratching 3
19	3	String scratching 4
20	4	Sixteenth notes
21	4	Sixteenth-note strum pattern 1
22	6	Open-chord fingerings
23	6	Barre-chord fingerings
24	6	Pentatonic-scale fingerings
25	6	Major-scale fingerings
26	6	Playing octaves
27	7	Hammer-ons, pull-offs, trills, and slides
28	7	Bending strings
29	7	Fretboard tapping
30	8	Playing natural harmonics
31	8	Plucking artificial harmonics
32	8	Playing pinch harmonics

(Continued)

Table A-2 (*Continued*)

Clip Number	Chapter	Description
33	9	Playing slide guitar
34	10	Alternate picking
35	10	Sweep picking and raking
36	10	Economy picking
37	11	Playing fingerpicking patterns
38	11	Playing chord melody
39	11	Using hybrid picking
40	11	Incorporating slapping
41	12	Using a tremolo system

Index

About the Author

Hailed as a "music-theory expert" by *Rolling Stone* magazine, guitarist **Desi Serna** is the author of the very popular *Fretboard Theory* line of guitar instructional material, as well as *Guitar Theory For Dummies*. He is known for his practical, hands-on approach to music teaching, with a focus on the guitar fretboard and emphasis on popular songs. Desi honed his craft through decades of teaching, performing, and publishing. He's online everyday posting lessons to `Guitar-Music-Theory.com` and discussing various guitar-music-related topics with his group of social media followers. In 2014, he relocated from his hometown of Toledo, Ohio, to an area near Nashville, Tennessee, to be closer to Music City and its community of guitar players.

Dedication

For everyone who bought a book, purchased a video, posted a positive review, and told a friend. I literally could not have done it without you!

Author's Acknowledgments

I want to extend a very special thanks to David Lutton for coordinating this project. I gratefully acknowledge all the folks at John Wiley & Sons, Inc., who had a hand in seeing this book through to completion, including Elizabeth Kuball and Sandy Williams. I also need to give credit to Thomas Evdokimoff for his added insight and Simon Revill for helping to create some of the figures. Above all else, I thank God for the gift of music and the opportunity to share it with others!

Publisher's Acknowledgments

Assistant Editor: David Lutton

Project Editor: Elizabeth Kuball

Copy Editor: Elizabeth Kuball

Technical Editor: Sandy Williams

Art Coordinator: Alicia B. South

Production Editor: Suresh Srinivasan

Cover Image: © PRSGuitars.com/Marc Quigley

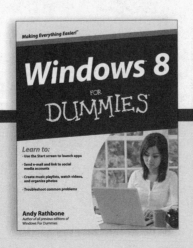

Anatomy and Physiology For Dummies, 2nd Edition
978-0-470-92326-9

Astronomy For Dummies, 3rd Edition
978-1-118-37697-3

Biology For Dummies, 2nd Edition
978-0-470-59875-7

Chemistry For Dummies, 2nd Edition
978-1-118-00730-3

1001 Algebra II Practice Problems For Dummies
978-1-118-44662-1

Microsoft Office

Excel 2013 For Dummies
978-1-118-51012-4

Office 2013 All-in-One For Dummies
978-1-118-51636-2

PowerPoint 2013 For Dummies
978-1-118-50253-2

Word 2013 For Dummies
978-1-118-49123-2

Music

Blues Harmonica For Dummies
978-1-118-25269-7

Guitar For Dummies, 3rd Edition
978-1-118-11554-1

iPod & iTunes For Dummies, 10th Edition
978-1-118-50864-0

Programming

Beginning Programming with C For Dummies
978-1-118-73763-7

Excel VBA Programming For Dummies, 3rd Edition
978-1-118-49037-2

Java For Dummies, 6th Edition
978-1-118-40780-6

Religion & Inspiration

The Bible For Dummies
978-0-7645-5296-0

Buddhism For Dummies, 2nd Edition
978-1-118-02379-2

Catholicism For Dummies, 2nd Edition
978-1-118-07778-8

Self-Help & Relationships

Beating Sugar Addiction For Dummies
978-1-118-54645-1

Meditation For Dummies, 3rd Edition
978-1-118-29144-3

Seniors

Laptops For Seniors For Dummies, 3rd Edition
978-1-118-71105-7

Computers For Seniors For Dummies, 3rd Edition
978-1-118-11553-4

iPad For Seniors For Dummies, 6th Edition
978-1-118-72826-0

Social Security For Dummies
978-1-118-20573-0

Smartphones & Tablets

Android Phones For Dummies, 2nd Edition
978-1-118-72030-1

Nexus Tablets For Dummies
978-1-118-77243-0

Samsung Galaxy S 4 For Dummies
978-1-118-64222-1

Samsung Galaxy Tabs For Dummies
978-1-118-77294-2

Test Prep

ACT For Dummies, 5th Edition
978-1-118-01259-8

ASVAB For Dummies, 3rd Edition
978-0-470-63760-9

GRE For Dummies, 7th Edition
978-0-470-88921-3

Officer Candidate Tests For Dummies
978-0-470-59876-4

Physician's Assistant Exam For Dummie
978-1-118-11556-5

Series 7 Exam For Dummies
978-0-470-09932-2

Windows 8

Windows 8.1 All-in-One For Dummies
978-1-118-82087-2

Windows 8.1 For Dummies
978-1-118-82121-3

Windows 8.1 For Dummies, Book + DVD Bundle
978-1-118-82107-7

e **Available in print and e-book formats.**

Available wherever books are sold. **For more information or to order direct visit www.dummies.com**

Take Dummies with you everywhere you go!

Whether you are excited about e-books, want more from the web, must have your mobile apps, or are swept up in social media, Dummies makes everything easier.

Leverage the Power

For Dummies is the global leader in the reference category and one of the most trusted and highly regarded brands in the world. No longer just focused on books, customers now have access to the For Dummies content they need in the format they want. Let us help you develop a solution that will fit your brand and help you connect with your customers.

Advertising & Sponsorships

Connect with an engaged audience on a powerful multimedia site, and position your message alongside expert how-to content.

Targeted ads • Video • Email marketing • Microsites • Sweepstakes sponsorship

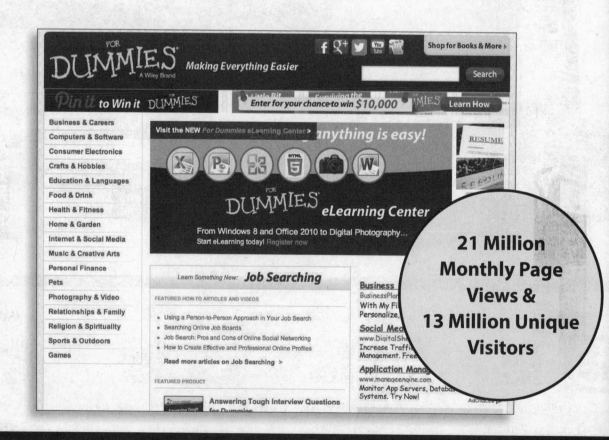

21 Million Monthly Page Views & 13 Million Unique Visitors

# of For Dummies

Custom Publishing

Reach a global audience in any language by creating a solution that will differentiate you from competitors, amplify your message, and encourage customers to make a buying decision.

Apps • Books • eBooks • Video • Audio • Webinars

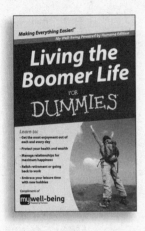   

Brand Licensing & Content

Leverage the strength of the world's most popular reference brand to reach new audiences and channels of distribution.

For more information, visit www.Dummies.com/biz

FOR DUMMIES
A Wiley Brand

Dummies products make life easier!

- DIY
- Consumer Electronics
- Crafts

- Software
- Cookware
- Hobbies

- Videos
- Music
- Games
- and More!

Dummies.com